CountryLiving

Pies&Tarts

CountryLiving

Pies & Tarts

HEARST
books

HEARSTBOOKS

An Imprint of Sterling Publishing
1166 Avenue of the Americas
New York, NY 10036

ISBN 978-1-61837-219-2

Distributed in Canada by Sterling Publishing
c/o Canadian Manda Group, 664 Annette Street
Toronto, Ontario, Canada M6S 2C8
Distributed in the United Kingdom by GMC Distribution Services
Castle Place, 166 High Street, Lewes, East Sussex, England BN7 1XU
Distributed in Australia by Capricorn Link (Australia) Pty. Ltd.
P.O. Box 704, Windsor, NSW 2756, Australia

For information about custom editions, special sales, and premium
and corporate purchases, please contact Sterling Special Sales at
800-805-5489 or specialsales@sterlingpublishing.com.

Manufactured in China

2 4 6 8 10 9 7 5 3 1

www.sterlingpublishing.com

Contents

Easy As Pie

PIES AND TARTS—staples of country cooking—made their way into American hearts long ago. In fact, nothing says "home sweet home" like the aroma of a freshly baked pie. Rolling and baking a golden-brown piecrust, then filling it with ripe seasonal fruit or a delectable savory filling, is always a pleasure. But the best part is sharing your homemade creation with friends and family. They will love digging into fresh-from-the-oven slices – plain, à la mode, or topped with a dollop of whipped cream.

Once upon a time, the art of making piecrusts was a basic skill taught to every young woman. Favorite family recipes were coveted, and pie-making tips and techniques were passed down from generation to generation. Unfortunately, many of us today have never been taught this skill, and if we have an archive of favorite family pie recipes, we are not confident in our ability to execute them. That means we rely all too frequently on bakeries to supply us with "homemade" pies for holidays and other special occasions.

This book aims to change that. We'll teach you the essentials of pie and tart making, then share more than seventy foolproof recipes—along with plenty of tips to help you along the way—so you can make your own pies from scratch with confidence. If you're an experienced pie baker, consider this a refresher course. You are likely to pick up some helpful techniques, along with more irresistible recipes to try. If you're new to pie-making, this book will be your tutor. Soon you'll be mixing, rolling, and baking beautiful homemade pies and tarts with ease!

So what are you waiting for?
Turn the page, and let's get baking!

BAKING FOR BEGINNERS

IF YOU ARE A NOVICE BAKER, HERE ARE SOME TIPS
THAT WILL HELP YOU FEEL AT HOME IN THE KITCHEN.

ALWAYS READ THE RECIPE THOROUGHLY BEFORE STARTING. Note the oven temperatures, cooking and baking times, and any specific equipment you may need. Before you start, gather all the required ingredients; do not make substitutions unless they are suggested in the recipe.

ACCURATE MEASUREMENTS ARE IMPORTANT IN BAKING. There are two types of measuring cups: those for dry ingredients (like flour and sugar) and those for liquids (such as water and milk). Dry measuring cups are usually made of metal or plastic and come in nested sets that include 1-cup, ½-cup, ⅓-cup, and ¼-cup sizes. Liquid measuring cups are usually made of glass or clear plastic and have a handle and spout for easy pouring; the measurements are marked on the side.

TO MEASURE DRY INGREDIENTS, start by stirring the ingredient in its container and then spoon it into a dry measuring cup. Level off the top with the straight-edge of a butter knife, holding the cup over the ingredient container. Then transfer the measured amount to your mixing bowl or sifter.

TO MEASURE LIQUIDS PROPERLY, pour the ingredient into a liquid measuring cup, place it on a level surface, and check the measurement at eye level.

BE CAREFUL WHEN WORKING AROUND HOT SURFACES, such as stovetop burners, ovens, and hot pans. Always have an oven mitt at the ready.

PREHEAT YOUR OVEN AS SPECIFIED, and don't be tempted to open the oven door during baking. It's important to maintain even heat during the baking process.

ALLOW YOUR PIE TO COOL AS SPECIFIED IN THE RECIPE. No pie should be served fresh out of the oven—hot fruit filling will burn your tongue! Set hot pie or tart pans on a wire rack to cool, so the air can circulate underneath. Depending on the recipe, the pie may be ready to serve when it has cooled just a bit or when it has reached room temperature—or you may need to chill it thoroughly. When it's time to serve soft meringue, custard, and cream pies, use a damp serrated knife, wiping the blade between each slice.

IF YOU WANT TO TRANSPORT YOUR PIE to a potluck, picnic, or maybe even a contest at a county fair, baker's boxes (found at restaurant supply and craft stores) are easy and economical. You can also purchase a reusable pie or cake carrier.

THE INGREDIENTS FOR SUCCESS

IF YOU WANT TO BECOME A SUCCESSFUL PIE BAKER, YOU
NEED TO START WITH TOP-QUALITY INGREDIENTS. HERE ARE
SOME TRIED-AND-TRUE TIPS TO HELP YOU PICK THE BEST.

FRUIT: If strawberries are in season, why bake an apple pie? For the most flavorful (not to mention affordable) pies, choose fruit that is fresh and at its seasonal peak. In the box opposite, we offer tips on selecting, sweetening, and peeling pie-perfect fruit. Don't have any fresh fruit on hand? If you have your heart set on a fruit pie, select a good-quality canned or frozen fruit that does not contain excessive amounts of sugar.

BUTTER: Butter is the key to sweet and delectable crusts, but some excellent recipes also include vegetable shortening for a flakier texture. Choose a brand of butter that you have come to trust, and be sure to check the sell-by dates to ensure freshness. It is critical that your butter be well chilled before you begin making the dough. Otherwise, you'll end up with an unwieldy crust that's difficult to work with and has an inferior texture after baking.

For the best results, freeze the butter pieces for a short while (20 to 30 minutes) before you begin, and then chop it into small pieces. If you have cool hands, rub the butter into the flour with your fingertips; if your hands are hot, it's best to use a pastry blender or two knives. After mixing, allow the dough to rest for at least 30 minutes to give the gluten time to relax. This makes the dough less elastic and easier to roll.

FLOUR: Most of the recipes in this book call for all-purpose flour. Choose a premium brand and store it at cool room temperature in a tightly sealed canister, tin, or plastic container to keep it fresh. Whole wheat flour is best stored in the freezer; if it's kept at room temperature, it can become rancid. The recipes in this book usually call for all-purpose flour. If you want to make your crust a little more tender, you can use all-purpose flour mixed with an equal weight of cake or pastry flour – a fine-textured, soft-wheat flour with a high starch content. Sift flour if the recipe directs it.

SUGAR: You'll need granulated, brown, and confectioners' sugar to make the recipes in this book. Store these in tightly-sealed containers to keep out humidity, which will cause them to clump.

FRUIT KNOW-HOW

Whether you pick it yourself or purchase it from a farmer's market or grocery store, here's how to get the most from your fruit.

GO FOR RIPE: Mature fruit at the height of the season is always the most flavorful. Smell, taste, and feel are all good indicators of ripeness.

SWEETEN WITH SUGAR: Some harvests will yield sweeter fruits than others, so taste to assess how much sugar you need to add. Sugar can work wonders to bring out the flavor in even slightly under-ripe fruits.

DON'T AUTOMATICALLY PEEL: The most intense flavor in a fruit is found in the peel, so if it's not tough, considering leaving the peel on when using fruits like peaches and plums.

USE YOUR FREEZER: To enjoy summer berries year-round, wash ripe berries in a colander and then set on paper towels to dry. Spread them in a single layer on baking sheets and freeze for 2 hours before transferring them to heavy-duty freezer bags. (Expel air from bags before freezing.)

TOOLS OF THE TRADE

YOU DON'T NEED AN ARSENAL OF FANCY TOOLS TO BAKE A PIE,
BUT HERE ARE SOME BASICS YOU'LL WANT TO HAVE ON-HAND.
MANY ARE ITEMS YOU PROBABLY ALREADY HAVE IN YOUR KITCHEN.
SOME, AS NOTED, YOU CAN DO WITHOUT.

BOWLS: A set of nesting bowls in graduated sizes from 1 to 3 quarts will see you through most pie-baking endeavors (or baking endeavors of any kind). Plastic bowls absorb fat, which is a problem when you need a grease-free bowl (for beating egg whites, for instance). Heatproof glass, ceramic, and stainless-steel bowls are all better choices. To keep a bowl from skating around the counter as you mix, place a damp kitchen towel or paper towels under it.

DRY AND LIQUID MEASURING CUPS: See our overview on page 8. You will also need a set of measuring spoons, which can be used for both dry and liquid ingredients.

WOODEN SPOONS AND A RUBBER SPATULA: Wooden spoons are gentle on dough and won't burn your fingers if you use them to stir hot pie fillings. Choose spoons made of hardwoods like maple; they should be smoothly finished and free of rough patches that might splinter off. You will also want a rubber spatula for scraping dough off the side of the bowl and getting every last drop of filling into the pie.

PASTRY BLENDER: If you find it difficult to cut butter or shortening into the flour mixture using two knives (and your hands are too hot!), try a pastry blender. Its straight handle is fitted with a curved sweep of tines or wires that make mixing pie dough easy. Look out for vintage versions at tag sales and flea markets.

ROLLING PIN: We recommend the kind with handles and a free-spinning roller. Choose a heavy rolling pin (at least 4 pounds); the weight itself will do most of the work, so you'll never have to lean into it. In a pinch, a wine bottle is a decent substitute for a rolling pin.

PIE PANS OR TINS: Made of ovenproof glass, ceramic, or metal, pie plates come in 8-, 9-, and 10-inch sizes. Crusts brown best in glass pans. Disposable pie pans are useful if you're baking a pie for a gift, but check the size—they often have a smaller capacity than durable pans.

TART PANS: These come in a wide range of sizes and shapes, from tiny 2-inch tartlets to huge 13-inch rounds. They can be square or rectangular, as well as circular. Many also come with removable bottoms, which is handy if you want to unmold your tart without risk of damage to the lovely golden-brown crust. If you want to stick with just one tart pan, get a simple 9-inch round one. It will allow you to prepare the majority of the tart recipes in this book.

PIE WEIGHTS: A piecrust baked blind (without the filling in it) needs to be weighted in the center to keep it from bubbling and buckling. Many bakers use dried beans for this purpose (and reuse them again and again). You can also purchase packets of small, bean-shaped aluminum pie weights. Line the bottom of the crust with aluminum foil or parchment before placing the weights on top.

COOLING RACKS: Pies and tarts should be cooled on a wire rack to allow the air to circulate underneath.

FOOD PROCESSOR: While certainly not necessary, a food processor makes mixing pie dough a breeze. Several recipes in this book provide instructions for doing just that. You'll need a metal blade attachment.

ESSENTIAL TECHNIQUES

MAKING A PIE (OR TART) CRUST IS EASIER THAN YOU THINK.
HERE, WE WALK YOU THROUGH THE PROCESS STEP-BY-STEP. INSTRUCTIONS
WILL VARY SLIGHTLY FROM RECIPE TO RECIPE, SO BE SURE TO READ
THROUGH THE RECIPE BEFORE YOU BEGIN.

MIX THE DOUGH: With a pastry blender (or two knives used scissor-fashion), "chop" the butter or shortening into the dry ingredients until crumb-like.

FLATTEN IT INTO A ROUND: Before rolling, let chilled dough stand at room temperature for 5 minutes. With a floured rolling pin on a floured surface, flatten the dough into a round.

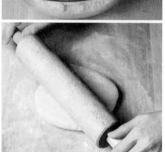

ROLL IT OUT: Roll out the dough to the size and thickness specified in the recipe (usually a couple inches larger than the pan size). Give the round an occasional quarter-turn as you roll; if it sticks, sprinkle the surface with a little flour.

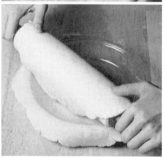

TRANSFER TO PAN: Fold half of the dough round over the rolling pin. Center the rolling pin over the pie or tart pan, and let the dough roll off the pin onto the pan. Pat the pie with your fingers so it conforms to the shape of the pan. To finish single-crust pies with decorative edges, see page 16. To shape a tart crust and finish the edges, see instructions on page 18.

BLIND BAKE: Recipes often instruct you to prebake (or "blind" bake) the crust before you add the filling. First, prick the bottom of the crust all over with a fork. This will help keep the crust from blistering as it bakes.

LINE WITH WEIGHTS: Next, line it with foil and fill it with dry beans, metal pie weights, or uncooked rice. This will prevent the crust from puffing up and shrinking as it bakes. Then, blind bake the crust for the time indicated in the recipe. If you are making a single crust pie or a tart, cool the prebaked shell, then fill it and bake for the time indicated in the recipe. If it's a double crust pie, see Add the Top Crust, next.

ADD THE TOP CRUST: If you are making a double-crust pie, cool the prebaked pie shell and then add the sweet or savory filling. Roll out the top crust and position on top of the pie, leaving a 1-inch overhang. Fold the edges under and seal them, then create a decorative edge, if you like (see page 16 for options).

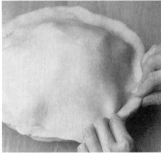

LET THE STEAM ESCAPE: Cut several 1-inch slits in the top of the pie to let steam escape, or create a decorative window (see page 17 for photo and directions). Then bake your pie for the time indicated in the recipe.

LET IT COOL: It's very important for air to circulate under a just-baked pie. Place it on a wire rack to cool for the recipe-recommended amount of time.

MAKING DECORATIVE BORDERS

ONCE YOU'VE MASTERED THE BASICS, ROLLING AND SHAPING A PIE CRUST
IS A RELAXING—AND REWARDING!—ENDEAVOR. HERE, WE PROVIDE
SOME IDEAS FOR DECORATIVE EDGES TO FINISH OFF YOUR PIES
WITH A TOUCH OF SIMPLE ARTISTRY.*

FORKED: This is the quickest, easiest border, but it gives piecrusts a finished look nonetheless. Using kitchen shears, trim the dough edge even with the rim of the pan. With floured fork tines, press the dough to the rim of the plate. Repeat all the way around to create a grooved pattern.

FLUTED: Using kitchen shears, trim the dough to leave a 1-inch overhang. Fold this under and pinch to make a stand-up edge. Push the tip of one index finger against the outside of the rim; with the index finger and thumb of your other hand, press to make a ruffle. Repeat all the way around, leaving about ¼ inch between the ruffles.

CRIMPED: Using kitchen shears, trim the dough to leave a 1-inch overhang. Fold this under and pinch to make a stand-up edge. Push the tip of one index finger against the inside of the rim; then pinch the dough by pressing with the index finger and thumb of your other hand. Repeat, moving your outer index finger into the impression made by your thumb.

TURRET: Using kitchen shears, trim the dough to leave a 1-inch overhang. Fold this under and pinch to make a stand-up edge. With a small knife, make cuts down through the edge to the rim of the pie, spacing cuts ½ inch apart. Fold pieces alternately toward the center and the rim.

HEARTS OR LEAVES: Using kitchen shears, trim the dough edge even with the rim of the pan. Gather the trimmings and roll them out to a ⅛-inch thickness. With a knife or tiny cookie cutter, cut out leaves or hearts of equal size. Lightly brush the edge of the piecrust with water, and then press the cutouts onto the edges all around the pie.

*NOTE: If the decorative pie edges appear to be over-browning in the oven, cover them with strips of aluminum foil, or create an aluminum foil circle that covers the crust only.

MAKING DECORATIVE PIE TOPS

HERE WE PROVIDE SOME CLEVER IDEAS FOR DECORATIVE TOPS
TO FINISH OFF YOUR PIES IN STYLE. THESE DESIGNS MAKE
ANY PIE LOOK BEAUTIFUL AND INTRICATE, BUT THE TECHNIQUES
ARE EASY TO MASTER!

WINDOW: Cut a 4-inch X in the center of the top crust; fold back the points to create a square opening. This window is not only decorative; it will also allow steam to escape from the pie during baking. Feel free to experiment with making windows in other whimsical shapes, such as the multiple tiny starts cut out of the top crust of our Strawberry Rhubarb Pie (page 62).

APPLIQUÉ: Roll out the reserved trimmings. Use a cookie cutter or a small knife to cut free-form shapes, such as fruits, hearts, or leaves (try using the back of the knife to mark veins on the leaves). Brush the cutouts with water and place them wet-side down on top of the pie. Cut several 1-inch slits in the top crust to allow steam to escape. The Quince Mince Pie (page 57) uses leaf-shaped appliqués cut from its own top crust as decoration.

SIMPLE LATTICE: Roll the second disk of dough into a 12-inch round, but instead of placing it over the filling, use a knife or fluted pastry wheel to cut it into ½-inch strips. Moisten the edge of the bottom crust with water. Place pastry strips about 1 inch apart across pie; press each strip at both ends to seal. Repeat with an equal number of strips placed at right angles to the first ones to create a lattice design. Turn overhang up over the ends of the strips and pinch to seal. Make a high, stand-up edge that will hold the juices in, and then flute the edge (see opposite page).

WOVEN LATTICE: Follow the instructions for the simple lattice above, but when you place the first layer of strips on the pie, do not seal the ends. Fold every other strip back halfway from the center of the pie. Place the center cross strip on the pie and replace the folded part of strips. Now fold back alternate strips; position second cross strip in place. Repeat until you've woven all the cross strips into a lattice pattern. Seal ends and make a high, fluted edge.

PIE BAKER'S CHEAT SHEET

If you're an experienced baker, you most likely have your own ideas about how to make a winning piecrust. But if you're new to the game, these pointers will help you turn out crusts you'll be proud to call your own.

FLAKINESS: Butter tastes better but melts faster than shortening. Use a tablespoon or two of shortening in place of the equal amount of butter to achieve a flakier crust. Also, be sure to keep your ingredients cold. If you have time, freeze them for about 20 minutes before you begin.

FIT: Lightly dusted parchment paper is the perfect rolling surface. If there's a chance your dough will get warm while you're rolling it, use parchment so you can easily transfer it to the refrigerator to re-chill. To fit the rolled-out circle of dough into the pie pan, center the rolling pin over the pie pan, then let the dough roll off the rolling pin onto the pan.

There's more to baking a pie than just popping it in the oven. Follow this advice to help your pie emerge from the oven looking gorgeous.

PREBAKE: If your piecrust will be filled with a moist filling, such as blueberries, the crust should be baked slightly before filling to prevent a soggy bottom. See page 15 for tips on weighting the crust before you prebake.

BAKE: Don't ruin a crust rim by burning it before the filling is cooked. Fit strips of aluminum foil around the pie edge to prevent overbrowning.

THE FINISH: If a pie is almost done baking but hasn't yet turned golden, mix an egg yolk with 1 tablespoon cream and lightly brush it over the crust. For a touch of sparkle, sprinkle with granulated sugar (this can also be done before you start baking). You can also use sanding sugar, found in baking supply stores, for more glitter.

PREPARING A TART CRUST

Tart pans are shallower than pie plates and typically feature fluted edges. Select a pan with a removable bottom—this will allow you to unmold the finished tart with ease. If you are just beginning, start out with a 9-inch round pan, the most common and versatile shape.

SHAPE THE CRUST: With a fluted tart pan, you don't have to worry about finishing the edges. Just press the dough gently into the rim so that it fills all the indentations. Let the dough hang loosely over the edge of the pan.

TRIM THE CRUST: To trim off the excess dough, simply roll a rolling pin over the edges of the pan; the rim will act as a cutting edge and the dough will fall away. Now you can blind bake your crust, or simply add the filling and bake it.

Master
Piecrust
Recipes

The Perfect Piecrust

MAKES TWO 9-INCH PIECRUSTS

3 cups all-purpose unbleached flour

1¼ teaspoons kosher salt

8 tablespoons (1 stick) cold butter, cubed

8 tablespoons cold shortening, cubed

10 to 12 tablespoons ice-cold lemon-lime soft drink (such as 7UP)

1. Pulse flour and salt in a food processor 3 or 4 times, or just until combined. Add butter and shortening, and pulse 8 to 10 times or just until mixture resembles small pebbles. Transfer mixture to a large mixing bowl. Add chilled soft drink, 1 tablespoon at a time, stirring with a fork until just combined.

2. Gently shape dough into 2 flat disks and wrap in plastic wrap. Transfer to a zip-top plastic bag and refrigerate for 8 hours or overnight (or freeze up to 3 months, if desired).

3. Preheat oven to 425°F.

4. Roll out dough on a lightly floured sheet of parchment paper to ¼-inch thickness (about a 12-inch circle). Fit into a 9-inch pie plate, crimping edges as desired. Refrigerate for 30 minutes to 1 hour.

5. Prick bottom of crust several times with a fork. Line with parchment and fill with pie weights. Bake for 15 minutes. Remove pie weights and bake 5 to 10 minutes more, or until golden. Remove to a wire rack and let cool completely.

Baked Pie Shell

1¼ **cups all-purpose flour**

¼ **teaspoon salt**

½ **cup (1 stick) unsalted butter, chilled and cut into small pieces**

4 to 6 **tablespoons ice water**

1. Combine the flour and salt in a large bowl. Cut in the butter using a pastry blender, 2 knives, or your fingers until the mixture resembles coarse meal. Sprinkle the ice water, 1 tablespoon at a time, over the flour mixture and mix with your hands or a fork until just combined. Transfer the dough to a clean, lightly floured work surface, gently gather it together, and flatten into a disk. Wrap the dough in plastic; chill for at least 1 hour or up to overnight. (The chilled dough may be frozen for up to 3 months.)

2. Preheat the oven to 450°F and position the rack in the center. On a lightly floured surface, roll the dough into a round, about ⅛-inch thick. Transfer the round to a 9-inch pie pan; gently fit it into the pan. Trim and finish the edge using one of the techniques described in Decorative Borders, page 17.

3. Prick the bottom and sides of the dough with a fork, then line it with parchment paper, and fill it with dried beans or pie weights. Bake the shell until it is lightly browned, 10 to 12 minutes. Transfer to a wire rack to cool completely.

Grandma's Pie Dough

MAKES 4 SINGLE CRUSTS

4 cups all-purpose flour

³/₄ teaspoon salt

1 tablespoon sugar

1³/₄ cups (3¹/₂ sticks) unsalted butter, chilled and cut into small pieces

1 tablespoon white vinegar

1 large egg

¹/₂ cup ice water

1. Combine the flour, salt, and sugar in a large bowl. Cut in the butter using a pastry blender, 2 knives, or your fingers until the mixture resembles coarse meal.

2. Whisk the vinegar, egg, and ice water together; mix the liquid into the flour mixture with your hands until just combined. Transfer the dough to a clean work surface and gently press to form a mass.

3. Divide the dough into 4 equal parts. Shape each into a disk and wrap it in plastic wrap. Chill for at least 1 hour, or freeze extras for up to 3 months.

Basic Pie Dough

MAKES 2 PIECRUSTS

2¹/₂ cups all-purpose flour, spooned and leveled

1 teaspoon kosher salt

1 teaspoon sugar

1 cup (2 sticks) cold unsalted butter, cut up

¹/₄ cup ice water

1. Whisk together flour, salt, and sugar. Cut in butter until it resembles coarse meal with several pea-size pieces remaining. Add water, 1 tablespoon at a time, using a fork to pull dough together into a crumbly pile (add up to an additional 2 tablespoons of water if needed).

2. Divide dough into two piles; wrap each in plastic wrap. Use the plastic to flatten and press dough into disks. Refrigerate until firm, 2 hours.

Quick Puff Pastry

2½ cups all-purpose flour, chilled

1 teaspoon salt

1½ cups (3 sticks) unsalted butter, frozen for 1 hour

¾ cup ice water

1. Fit a food processor with the largest of the grater attachments or freeze a metal box grater with large holes. Combine the flour and salt; set aside. Quickly grate the butter and add it to the flour mixture. Re-chill the butter and flour if necessary. Add the ice water to the bowl and stir until just combined – the dough will be a loose, shaggy mass.

2. Transfer the dough to a well-floured surface; roll and shape it into a long 6″ by 18″ rectangle. Using a large spatula, fold or flip the bottom portion of the dough toward the middle and bring the top part of the dough down-ward to the edge, as if you were folding a business letter. Rotate the dough a quarter turn to the right so that the shorter end of the dough is closer to you, and roll it out again into a 6″ by 18″ rectangle.

3. Repeat the folding and turning, then roll out the dough and fold it once more. Wrap the dough in plastic wrap and refrigerate for at least 30 minutes or up to 24 hours. The dough can also be wrapped in plastic and frozen for up to 2 months.

Crumb Crust Three Ways
Graham Cracker · Gingersnap · Vanilla Wafer

MAKES ONE 9-INCH PIECRUST

1½ cups fine cookie crumbs

2 tablespoons sugar

5 tablespoons butter or margarine, melted

1. Preheat the oven to 375°F. In a medium bowl, with a fork, stir crumbs and sugar with melted butter until evenly blended and moistened. With your hand, press the mixture onto the bottom and up the sides of a 9-inch pie pan or 9-inch tart pan with removable bottom.

2. Bake the crust for 8 to 10 minutes. Cool completely on a wire rack.

Fruit Pies

Rustic Strawberry Galette

This simple summer recipe allows the strawberries to shine. A hint of vanilla and lemon is folded into the mix and awaits beneath a crispy, sweet crust.

MAKES 6 SLICES

1¼ cups all-purpose flour, plus more for work surface

¼ teaspoon salt

1 tablespoon plus ¼ cup granulated sugar

½ package cream cheese (4 ounces), cut into ½-inch cubes

2 pounds strawberries, hulled and halved (large ones quartered)

1 tablespoon cornstarch

1 vanilla bean, seeds scraped and reserved (pod discarded)

1 teaspoon lemon zest

1 egg, beaten with 1 teaspoon water

2 tablespoons turbinado sugar

1. In a food processor, pulse flour, salt, and 1 tablespoon granulated sugar to combine. Add cream cheese and butter and pulse until large crumbs form. Add 3 to 4 tablespoons water and pulse just until dough begins to come together. Turn dough out onto a lightly floured work surface and gently knead until dough comes together evenly. Pat into a disk and wrap tightly in plastic wrap. Refrigerate for at least 1 hour or up to overnight.

2. Unwrap dough disk and roll between 2 sheets of parchment to create a 12-inch-diameter circle that is ⅛-inch thick. Transfer dough to a baking sheet and refrigerate for 30 minutes.

3. Preheat oven to 350°F. Meanwhile, in a large bowl, toss strawberries with cornstarch, vanilla-bean seeds, lemon zest, and remaining granulated sugar. Arrange strawberries atop dough, leaving a 1-inch border. Fold border up and over strawberries to create a 1-inch-wide rim. Brush crust with egg wash and sprinkle with turbinado sugar. Bake galette until crust is golden, 40 to 45 minutes.

LIGHTEN UP!

Reduce all-purpose flour to ½ cup and add ¾ cup whole wheat flour. Replace cream cheese with 6 ounces of low-fat variety. Reduce butter to ¼ stick and cut turbinado sugar. **Total savings:** 133 calories and 13 grams of fat.

Blueberry-Peach Lattice Pie

Make the most of two beloved summer fruits—succulent blueberries and juicy, sweet peaches—by baking this luscious pie topped with a pretty lattice crust.

MAKES: ONE 10-INCH PIE

CRUST

2 1/2 cups all-purpose flour

3/4 cup sugar

1/2 teaspoon salt

14 tablespoons unsalted butter, chilled and cut into small pieces

1/2 teaspoon pure vanilla extract

3 to 5 tablespoons ice water

FILLING

1 pint (2 cups) fresh blueberries, stems removed

3 cups peeled, sliced fresh peaches

3/4 cup plus 1 tablespoon sugar

3 tablespoons cornstarch

1/2 teaspoon ground cinnamon

1/2 teaspoon grated lemon zest

1 large egg, lightly beaten

1. **For the crust:** In a large bowl, combine the flour, sugar, and salt. Cut in the butter using a pastry blender, 2 knives, or your fingers until the mixture resembles coarse meal. Using a fork, mix in the vanilla; then add the water 1 tablespoon at a time, just until the mixture begins to cling together. Gather the dough into a ball, divide it in half, and flatten each piece into a disk. Wrap the disks tightly in plastic and refrigerate for 1 hour or up to overnight.

2. Preheat the oven to 425°F and position the rack in the center. On a floured surface, roll 1 pastry disk into a 12-inch-diameter round. Transfer to a 10-inch pie pan. Trim the dough, leaving a 1/2-inch overhang. Fold the overhanging pastry under and pinch the dough to crimp around the rim. Cut out a circle of parchment paper to cover the bottom of the dough and line it with pie weights or dried beans. Bake the shell for 10 minutes. Transfer to a wire rack and remove the weights and paper. Lower the oven temperature to 375°F.

3. Remove the remaining pastry disk from the refrigerator. On a floured surface, roll it into a thin circle. Use a pizza wheel or fluted pastry cutter to cut 10 strips, each about 1-inch wide. Transfer the strips to a parchment-lined baking sheet, cover them with plastic wrap, and chill until ready to use.

4. **Make the filling and assemble the pie:** In a large bowl, combine the blueberries and peaches. In a small bowl, combine 3/4 cup sugar with the cornstarch, cinnamon, and lemon zest. Add the cornstarch mixture to the fruit and gently toss to coat. Pour the filling into the baked piecrust. Weave the reserved pastry strips into a lattice pattern over the fruit (see page 16). Lightly brush the lattice with beaten egg and sprinkle with the remaining 1 tablespoon sugar.

5. Loosely cover the crimped edge of the crust with foil to prevent overbrowning. Bake the pie until the filling bubbles and the crust is golden brown, about 45 minutes. Transfer to a wire rack to cool completely.

Cherry-Berry Jumble Fruit Pie

Who says less is more? Together with sweet cherries, four different berries—strawberries, blueberries, blackberries, and raspberries—elevate this stellar pie (inspired by the 2006 North Carolina State Fair winner) to new flavor heights.

MAKES ONE 9-INCH PIE

Perfect Piecrust (page 22), unbaked

³/₄ cup sugar

2 tablespoons cornstarch

1 tablespoon all-purpose flour

1 cup canned sweet cherries (one 15-ounce can)

1¹/₂ cups fresh sliced strawberries

1¹/₄ cups fresh blueberries

³/₄ cup fresh blackberries

¹/₂ cup fresh raspberries

1 tablespoon fresh lemon juice

1. Roll out half the dough on a lightly floured sheet of parchment paper to ¹/₄-inch thickness (about a 12-inch circle). Fit into a 9-inch pie plate, crimping edges as desired. Refrigerate 30 minutes to 1 hour.

2. Preheat oven to 375°F.

3. Whisk together sugar, cornstarch, and flour. Stir together sugar mixture, fruit, and lemon juice. Pour into prepared crust.

4. Roll out remaining dough disk to about ¹/₄-inch thickness on a lightly floured surface. Cut dough into 9 (1-inch-wide) strips. Arrange strips in a lattice design over filling; gently press ends of strips into bottom crust. Crimp edge of crust.

5. Bake at 375°F for 1 hour, or until lightly brown and bubbly. Cover with foil, if necessary, to prevent excess browning.

Classic Blueberry Pie

A homemade pie will take pride of place at any picnic. This irresistible blueberry pie—
perfect for the Fourth of July—uses a mix of butter and vegetable shortening for the crust.
Instead of venting the pie with slits, a decorative star shape is cut out of the top crust.

MAKES: ONE 10-INCH PIE

4 1/4 cups all-purpose flour

1 cup plus 2 tablespoons sugar

1/2 teaspoon salt

1 1/4 cups unsalted butter, chilled and cubed

1/4 cup vegetable shortening, chilled

1 teaspoon vinegar

3/4 cup ice water

3 pints fresh blueberries, stems removed

1/2 teaspoon freshly grated ginger

1/2 teaspoon lemon zest

1 tablespoon fresh lemon juice

1 tablespoon heavy cream

1. Combine the flour, 1/4 cup sugar, and salt in a large bowl. Cut in the butter and shortening using a pastry blender, 2 knives, or your fingers until the mixture resembles coarse meal. Add the vinegar and the water, sprinkling in a few tablespoons at a time as necessary (you may not need it all), and mix until just combined. Gather the dough into a ball, divide it in two, and form each half into a disk. Wrap the disks tightly in plastic wrap and chill for at least 1 hour or overnight.

2. Preheat the oven to 425°F. On a lightly floured surface, between two sheets of waxed paper, roll 1 pastry disk into a round at least 12 inches in diameter and 1/16-inch thick. Transfer the dough to a 10-inch pie plate and trim, leaving a 1/2-inch overhang; fold under and pinch the dough to crimp around the rim. Line the shell with parchment paper and fill with it dried beans or pie weights. Bake until lightly browned, about 10 minutes. Remove the beans and paper and bake the shell for 10 minutes longer. Transfer to a wire rack to cool completely. Reduce the oven temperature to 400°F. Roll the second pastry disk to the same size as the first and place it on a baking sheet lined with waxed paper. Cover and refrigerate both parts of the crust.

3. Toss the blueberries with the ginger, lemon zest and juice, and 3/4 cup sugar in a large bowl. Transfer the filling to the prepared crust. Using a small star-shaped cookie cutter, cut a ventilation hole in the center of the top crust, then drape the dough over the filling, taking care not to stretch the star hole out of shape; crimp the edges of the crust to seal them. Lightly brush the top crust with the cream and sprinkle on the remaining 2 tablespoons sugar. Loosely cover the crimped edge of the crust with strips of foil to prevent overbrowning. Bake the pie for 15 minutes, then reduce the oven temperature to 375°F and continue baking until the blueberry filling bubbles and crust is golden brown, about 45 minutes. Transfer to a wire rack to cool completely.

Farmhouse Apple Pie

This is the sort of apple pie Grandma used to make—that is, if you were lucky!
Enjoy it warm or cold, unembellished or à la mode.

MAKES ONE 9-INCH PIE

½ **recipe (2 disks)
Grandma's Pie Dough
(page 25)**

2½ **pounds mixed apples,
peeled, cored, and chopped into
¾-inch pieces**

2 tablespoons all-purpose flour

¾ **cup plus 1 tablespoon sugar**

1 teaspoon ground cinnamon

¼ **teaspoon ground nutmeg**

½ **teaspoon salt**

1 tablespoon fresh lemon juice

1. Preheat the oven to 375°F. On a lightly floured surface, roll the disks of dough into rounds about ⅛-inch thick; transfer one to a 9-inch pie pan (see Tip). Place the remaining round on a baking sheet lined with parchment paper; keep both dough pieces chilled.

2. Toss the apples, flour, ¾ cup sugar, cinnamon, nutmeg, salt, and lemon juice together and mix until combined. Pour the apple mixture into the prepared pie pan and place the top dough round over it. Trim the edges of the dough, leaving a ½-inch overhang; fold under and crimp the edges. Sprinkle the top of the pie with the remaining 1 tablespoon sugar; chill for 10 minutes.

3. Bake until the fruit is bubbling and the crust is golden brown, 50 to 55 minutes. Transfer to a wire rack to cool completely.

TIP

Drape the dough over the rolling pin and unroll it onto the pie pan to prevent tearing.

Pear Crumb Pie

Inspired by the winner at the 2010 Iowa State Fair, this fresh fruit pie has a delicious surprise in the filling—cranberries! Serve warm with a scoop of vanilla ice cream, if you like.

MAKES ONE 9-INCH PIE

Perfect Piecrust (page 22), unbaked

3/4 cup plus 1/3 cup all-purpose flour

1/2 cup cold butter, cubed

3/4 cup light brown sugar

1/2 cup old-fashioned oats

1/2 cup chopped toasted pecans

1 cup sugar

2 teaspoons cinnamon

6 cups peeled and sliced Bartlett pears (2 1/2 pounds)

1/2 cup dried cranberries

1. Roll out half the dough on a lightly floured sheet of parchment paper to 1/4-inch thickness (about a 12-inch circle). Fit into a 9-inch pie plate, crimping edges as desired. Refrigerate 30 minutes to 1 hour.

2. Preheat oven to 365°F.

3. Cut butter into 3/4 cup flour using a pastry blender or fork until mixture resembles coarse meal. Stir in brown sugar, oats, and pecans; set mixture aside.

4. Stir together 1/3 cup flour, sugar, and cinnamon. Add pears and cranberries, stirring to coat. Pour into prepared crust. Top evenly with pecan mixture. Place on an aluminum foil-lined rimmed baking sheet.

5. Bake at 365°F for 70 minutes, or until bubbly and golden brown. Let cool completely on wire rack.

Mixed Berry Crostata

This free-form tart is simple to make and very adaptable. You can substitute equal amounts of peaches, plums, or apricots for the berries, or use half berries and half stone fruits.

MAKES ONE 8-INCH CROSTATA

1¼ cups plus 1 tablespoon all-purpose flour

¼ cup plus 2 tablespoons granulated sugar

⅛ teaspoon salt

½ cup (1 stick) unsalted butter, softened

2 large eggs

1 cup fresh raspberries

1 cup fresh blackberries

1 tablespoon fresh lemon juice

1 tablespoon turbinado sugar (optional)

1. **Make the pastry:** Combine 1¼ cups flour, ¼ cup granulated sugar, and salt in a large bowl. Lightly beat one of the eggs. Form a well in the center of the dry ingredients and place the butter and beaten egg in the well. Using your hands, mix the ingredients into a soft, pliable dough. Mold into a 4-inch disk and place it on a lightly floured sheet of parchment paper. Lightly dust the dough with flour and roll it into a 10-inch circle. Place the dough, still on the parchment, on a baking sheet, cover it with plastic wrap, and chill for 10 minutes. Preheat the oven to 375°F and position the rack in the middle.

2. **Assemble the crostata:** In a small bowl, mix the remaining flour and granulated sugar; set aside. Evenly sprinkle the flour-and-sugar mixture on the dough, leaving a 1-inch-wide border around the edge. Place berries on top of the mixture and sprinkle with lemon juice. Fold the border over the top of the berries to form an 8-inch tart.

3. **Bake the crostata:** Beat the remaining egg and lightly brush the top of the dough border with the mixture; sprinkle with turbinado sugar, if desired. Bake for about 35 minutes. Slide the crostata, on the parchment paper, onto a wire rack, and let cool for 1 hour. Serve warm or at room temperature.

Rustic Apple-Pomegranate Tart

A pomegranate glaze dresses up this rustic apple tart.
Cinnamon scents the dough.

CINNAMON PASTRY

1½ cups all-purpose flour, unsifted

2 teaspoons sugar

1 teaspoon ground cinnamon

¼ teaspoon salt

½ cup (1 stick) unsalted butter, chilled

1 large egg

3 tablespoons ice water

FILLING

2 tablespoons unsalted butter

3 large Granny Smith apples, peeled, cored, and sliced into ⅛-inch-thick pieces

3 large Golden Delicious apples, peeled, cored, and sliced into ⅛-inch-thick pieces

¼ cup sugar

⅛ teaspoon salt

GLAZE

1 large pomegranate

¼ cup sugar

1 tablespoon fresh lemon juice

1. **Prepare the cinnamon pastry:** In a medium bowl, combine the flour, sugar, cinnamon, and salt. Cut in the butter with a pastry blender, 2 knives, or your fingers until the mixture resembles very coarse crumbs. In a cup, use a fork to beat the egg and ice water until well combined. Measure 1 tablespoon egg mixture into another cup and set aside. Add the remaining egg mixture to the flour mixture, tossing lightly with a fork until the pastry is moist enough to hold together. Wrap and set the pastry aside at room temperature until you are ready to assemble the tart.

2. **Prepare the filling:** In a large heavy skillet, melt the butter. Add the apples and cook, stirring constantly, until they are just tender and most of the liquid has evaporated. Stir in the sugar and salt; set aside to cool slightly.

3. Preheat the oven to 375°F. Between one sheet of parchment paper or heavy-duty aluminum foil and one sheet of waxed paper, roll out the floured pastry to a 15-inch round. Remove the waxed paper; place the pastry, still on the parchment, onto a rimmed baking sheet.

4. Transfer the filling to the center of the pastry, leaving a 3-inch border. Fold the edges of the pastry over the filling. Brush the pastry with the reserved egg mixture. Bake for 35 minutes, or until brown and bubbling. Transfer the tart, on the parchment, to a wire rack to cool completely.

5. **While the tart bakes, prepare the glaze:** Quarter the pomegranate and remove the seeds from the membrane; discard the shell and membrane. Set aside 3 tablespoons of the seeds. Place the remaining seeds in a blender and liquefy. Pour the pomegranate juice through a strainer into a 1-quart saucepan. Add the sugar and lemon juice, and heat to boiling. Cook for 5 minutes or until thickened. Sprinkle the reserved seeds over the apple filling in the still-warm tart and drizzle glaze over all. Let cool to room temperature before serving.

Yogurt and Fruit Tartlets with Cereal Crusts

These crisp tart shells are made with crushed cereal, almonds, and maple syrup and require just 10 minutes to bake. Yogurt makes a creamy, high-calcium filling. Top with your choice of berries or sliced fruit.

MAKES 8 TARTLETS

5 cups cornflakes

1 cup pecan halves

4 tablespoons (½ stick) unsalted butter, melted

6 tablespoons maple syrup

1 (16-ounce) container vanilla yogurt

2⅔ cups fresh fruit (such as grapes, blueberries, and raspberries)

1. Preheat the oven to 350°F. Place eight 4-inch round tart pans with removable bottoms on a baking sheet; set aside. In the bowl of a food processor fitted with a metal blade, process the cornflakes and pecans until combined, about 10 short pulses. Transfer the crumb mixture to a large bowl, drizzle it with the melted butter, and toss to combine. Stir in the maple syrup. Evenly divide the cereal mixture among the tart pans; press into the bottoms and along sides to form shells. Bake for 10 minutes. Transfer to a wire rack to cool completely.

2. Remove each shell from its mold and transfer to a serving plate. Mix up the yogurt and top each tart shell with ¼ cup yogurt and ⅓ cup fruit. Serve immediately.

Cranberry Turnovers

These tasty turnovers require only five ingredients and are so simple to put together.
A sweet drizzle of icing is the perfect finishing touch.

8 ounces cream cheese, softened

2 egg yolks

2 cups confectioners' sugar

1 (17.3-ounce) package puff pastry, thawed

³/₄ cup cranberry sauce

1. Preheat oven to 400°F. In a medium bowl and using an electric mixer set on low, beat cream cheese, egg yolks, and 1 cup confectioners' sugar until smooth, 2 to 3 minutes. Set aside.

2. Roll out 1 puff pastry sheet into a 10-inch square; cut into four 5-inch squares. Place 2 tablespoons cream-cheese mixture in center of each square. Top each with 1½ tablespoons cranberry sauce. Dampen edges of each square with water and fold over to form a triangle. Press edges together with a fork to seal. Transfer turnovers to a parchment-lined baking pan. Repeat with second puff pastry sheet to make remaining turnovers.

3. Bake turnovers until puffed and golden brown, about 20 minutes. Transfer turnovers to a wire rack to cool, about 10 minutes.

4. In a small bowl, stir together remaining confectioners' sugar and 4 tablespoons water until a thick but flowing icing forms. (If icing is too thick, add more water, a few drops at a time.) Fill a resealable plastic bag with icing, seal bag, and snip off a tiny corner. Pipe icing over turnovers.

Peach-Huckleberry Lattice Pie

This lovely lattice crust creates a patchwork of colors and textures, a pleasing pattern of baked fruit peeking from beneath strips of tender pastry. Huckleberries are wild, blue-black berries that resemble blueberries, but are more tart in flavor. They are in-season from June through August.

MAKES ONE 9-INCH PIE

½ **recipe (2 disks) Grandma's Pie Dough (page 25)**

5 cups 1-inch peach slices (from about 5 medium peaches)

½ cup fresh huckleberries

¾ cup sugar

¼ cup all-purpose flour

½ teaspoon ground cinnamon

1. Preheat the oven to 400°F. On a lightly floured surface, roll a disk of dough into a ⅛-inch-thick round. Transfer to a 9-inch pie pan and trim the edges, leaving a ½-inch overhang. Set the shell aside and keep chilled. Roll the remaining disk of dough into a round the same size as the first. Cut ten 1-inch strips using a pizza wheel or fluted pastry cutter. Lay the strips on a parchment paper-lined baking sheet, cover with plastic wrap, and chill until ready to use.

2. Toss the peaches, huckleberries, sugar, flour, and cinnamon together in a large bowl. Pour the filling into the prepared pie shell. Weave the pastry strips into a lattice pattern over the fruit (see page 16). Chill the pie for 10 minutes, then bake until the fruit is bubbling and the crust is golden brown, 50 to 55 minutes. Transfer to a wire rack to cool completely.

Cherry-Walnut Turnovers

Crisp phyllo pastry envelops a dried cherry-and-walnut filling drenched with spicy cherry syrup. To enjoy every last bite, serve with a scoop of vanilla ice cream.

MAKES 10 TURNOVERS

2 cups walnuts, toasted and chopped

1 cup dried cherries, chopped

½ cup Spiced Cherry Syrup (recipe below)

2 tablespoons honey

1 teaspoon grated lemon zest

½ teaspoon salt

20 frozen phyllo sheets, thawed

½ cup (1 stick) unsalted butter, melted

½ cup confectioners' sugar

1. Combine the walnuts, dried cherries, syrup, honey, lemon zest, and salt in a medium bowl; set aside. Preheat the oven to 375°F. Line a baking sheet with parchment paper.

2. Lay the phyllo on a clean, flat surface and cover the stack with a damp dish towel. Place one sheet of phyllo on your work surface and brush it with melted butter. Sprinkle it with about 1 teaspoon confectioners' sugar, top it with another phyllo sheet, brush again with butter, and sprinkle with sugar.

3. Place about ¼ cup cherry-walnut filling in the bottom center of the phyllo, about 1 inch from the edge. Fold each phyllo strip around the filling into a triangle shape, as you would fold a flag.

4. Transfer the turnover to the prepared baking sheet and brush the surface with melted butter. Using the remaining ingredients, repeat the filling and folding process. Bake the turnovers until they are golden brown and crisp, about 15 minutes. Transfer to a wire rack to cool completely. They will keep in an airtight container for up to 2 days.

SPICED CHERRY SYRUP

MAKES ABOUT 1 CUP

3 cups (about 1 pound) sweet cherries, pitted and halved

¼ cup water

¼ cup sugar

1 tablespoon fresh lemon juice

4 sticks cinnamon

Peel of 1 lemon, white pith removed, cut into 1-inch pieces

1. In a medium saucepan over medium-high heat, combine the cherries, water, sugar, lemon juice, cinnamon sticks, and lemon peel; bring to a boil. Reduce the heat and simmer until the cherries soften, 10 to 15 minutes.

2. Remove the cinnamon sticks and lemon zest and run the mixture through a food mill into a medium bowl. Strain through a fine sieve. Transfer the syrup to an airtight container and refrigerate for up to 3 days.

Raspberry and Fig Tart

The sublime flavor of fresh figs plays off the tang of
red raspberries in this sophisticated almond-crust tart.

ALMOND CRUST

1 cup all-purpose flour, unsifted

½ cup ground natural almonds

2 tablespoons sugar

¼ teaspoon salt

½ cup (1 stick) unsalted butter, chilled and cut into small pieces

1 teaspoon almond extract

2 to 4 tablespoons ice water

FILLING

⅓ cup seedless red-raspberry preserves

2 tablespoons fresh lemon juice

6 large fresh figs (about 8 ounces)

1 cup (½ pint) fresh red raspberries

Fresh mint sprigs, for garnish (optional)

1. **For the almond crust:** In a medium bowl, combine the flour, almonds, sugar, and salt. Cut in the butter using a pastry blender, 2 knives, or your fingers until the mixture resembles coarse meal. Sprinkle in the almond extract; add the ice water, 1 tablespoon at a time, tossing lightly with a fork until the pastry is moist enough to hold together when lightly pressed. Shape the pastry into a disk. Wrap it in plastic wrap and refrigerate for 30 minutes. Preheat the oven to 375°F.

2. Between 2 sheets of floured waxed paper, roll the chilled pastry into a 12-inch round. Remove the top sheet of waxed paper and invert the pastry into a 9½-inch tart pan with a removable bottom, allowing the excess to extend over the edge. Peel off the remaining sheet of waxed paper. Fold the excess pastry inward so that the crust is even with the rim of the pan. Press the pastry against the sides to make an even thickness. With a fork, pierce the bottom of the pastry crust to prevent shrinkage and bubbling. Line the crust with a piece of aluminum foil, allowing it to extend over the edge of the crust, and fill with pie weights or dried beans.

3. Bake the crust for 10 minutes, then remove the foil with the beans and bake until crisp and golden, 12 to 15 minutes more. Transfer to a wire rack to cool completely.

4. **Prepare the filling:** No more than 1 hour before serving, combine the preserves and lemon juice in a small bowl; set aside. Cut the figs lengthwise in half. With a pastry brush, spread 2 tablespoons of the preserve mixture evenly over the bottom of the crust. Arrange 8 fig halves, cut-sides up, around the edge of the crust with the stems toward the center. Place the remaining 4 fig halves in the center with the stems pointing out.

5. Place 3 large berries in the center of the tart. Arrange the remaining berries in the spaces between the figs. Brush the remaining preserve mixture over the figs and berries.

6. Remove the rim of the pan from the tart. Place the tart on a serving plate and garnish with mint sprigs, if desired.

Apple-Cheddar Crumble Pie

This single-crust pie is finished with a Cheddar cheese-enriched crumble topping. Choose an assortment of tart and sweet apple varieties to yield a heavenly-perfumed pie.

CRUST

1¼ cups all-purpose flour

½ teaspoon salt

⅛ teaspoon cayenne pepper

½ cup (1 stick) unsalted butter, chilled and cut into pieces

¾ cup grated sharp Cheddar cheese

3 to 4 tablespoons ice water

FILLING

3 medium tart apples, such as Rhode Island Greening, Cortland, or Granny Smith, peeled, cored, and thinly sliced (3 cups)

3 medium sweet apples, such as Rome Beauty or Jonathan, peeled, cored, and thinly sliced (3 cups)

1 teaspoon grated lemon zest

¼ cup fresh lemon juice (from about 2 lemons)

¾ cup sugar

2 tablespoons all-purpose flour

½ teaspoon ground cinnamon

¼ teaspoon salt

¼ teaspoon ground nutmeg

⅛ teaspoon ground allspice

CRUMBLE TOPPING

⅓ cup all-purpose flour

3 tablespoons brown sugar, packed

3 tablespoons unsalted butter, chilled and cut into small pieces

½ cup grated sharp Cheddar cheese

1. **For the crust:** In a large bowl, combine the flour, salt, and cayenne pepper. Cut in the butter using a pastry blender, 2 knives, or your fingers until the mixture resembles coarse meal. Add the cheese and toss. Add the ice water, 1 tablespoon at a time, until a rough dough forms. Gather the dough together, shape it into a ¾-inch-thick disk, and wrap tightly in plastic wrap. Refrigerate for 30 minutes.

2. On a lightly floured surface, roll the dough into an 11-inch circle, about ¼-inch thick. Gently fit into a 9-inch pie pan, turn the overhanging dough under to form an edge along the top of the pan, and crimp the edge. Chill for 30 minutes.

3. Preheat the oven to 425°F and place the rack in the center position. Line the crust with parchment paper and fill with pie weights or dried beans. Bake until the crust is lightly browned, about 15 minutes. Transfer to a wire rack and remove the weights and paper. Leave the oven on.

4. **For the filling:** In a large bowl, toss all the apple slices with the lemon zest and juice. In a small bowl, mix the sugar, flour, cinnamon, salt, nutmeg, and allspice. Sprinkle the spice mixture over the apples and toss to coat thoroughly. Spoon the apples into the prepared crust.

5. **For the crumble topping:** In a small bowl, with a fork, toss together the flour, brown sugar, butter, and grated cheese. Sprinkle the top of the pie with the crumble mixture.

6. Bake the pie until the topping is golden brown, 50 to 60 minutes. Transfer to a wire rack to cool for at least 30 minutes. Serve warm or at room temperature.

Raspberry-Almond Tart

Bright, beautiful raspberries adorn the top of this creamy nutty tart.
Once assembled, add a dusting of powdered sugar for extra elegance.

CRUST

1½ **cups all-purpose flour**

½ **teaspoon salt**

½ **cup (1 stick) cold butter, cut up**

2 **tablespoons vegetable shortening**

FILLING

1 **tube or can (7 to 8 ounces) almond paste, broken into 1-inch pieces**

4 **tablespoons butter, softened**

½ **cup sugar**

¼ **teaspoon salt**

2 **large eggs**

2 **teaspoons vanilla extract**

¼ **cup all-purpose flour**

1½ **cups raspberries**

1. **Prepare the tart crust:** In medium bowl, mix flour and salt. With pastry blender or two knives used scissor-fashion, cut into butter with shortening until mixture resembles coarse crumbs. Add 5 to 6 tablespoons cold water, 1 tablespoon at a time, mixing lightly with fork after each addition, until dough is just moist enough to hold together. Shape dough into a disk; wrap in plastic wrap and refrigerate for 30 minutes.

2. On a lightly floured surface, with floured rolling pin, roll dough into a 14-inch round. Ease dough round into an 11-inch round tart pan with removable bottom. Fold overhang in and press against side of tart pan to form a rim ⅛-inch above the edge of the pan. Refrigerate for 15 minutes to firm pastry slightly before baking.

3. Preheat oven to 375°F. Line tart shell with foil and fill with pie weights, dried beans, or uncooked rice. Bake tart shell for 20 minutes; remove foil with weights and bake 8 to 10 minutes more, or until golden. Transfer pan to wire rack.

4. **Meanwhile, prepare the filling:** In large bowl, with mixer at medium speed, beat almond paste, butter, sugar, and salt until evenly blended, scraping bowl frequently with rubber spatula (mixture will resemble coarse crumbs). Add eggs and vanilla. Increase speed to medium-high and beat until blended. (It's okay if there are tiny lumps.) With spoon, stir in flour.

5. Pour almond mixture into warm tart shell; spread evenly. Place raspberries in an even layer over filling. Bake tart 40 to 50 minutes, until golden. Cool tart in pan on wire rack. When cool, carefully remove side from pan.

Fresh Berry Crumble Pie

This deep-dish summer berry pie features a hazelnut crust and a brown-sugar hazelnut crumb topping. Top with a dollop of whipped cream for a dessert worthy of a county fair ribbon.

MAKES ONE 9-INCH DEEP-DISH PIE

13 tablespoons unsalted butter, chilled and cubed

1³⁄₄ cups confectioners' sugar, sifted

1 cup hazelnuts, finely ground

¹⁄₄ teaspoon salt

¹⁄₂ teaspoon pure vanilla extract

1 large egg

2 cups all-purpose flour

3 quarts strawberries, hulled and halved

1 tablespoon fresh lemon juice

3 tablespoons cornstarch

¹⁄₂ pint (1 cup) raspberries

¹⁄₄ cup light brown sugar

1. In the bowl of a mixer fitted with the paddle attachment, beat 10 tablespoons butter on high speed until creamy. Reduce the speed to low and add 1 cup confectioners' sugar and ¹⁄₂ cup hazelnuts, along with the salt, vanilla, and egg; beat until smooth. Add 1²⁄₃ cups flour in 3 additions, mixing until just combined. Gather the dough into a ball, wrap in plastic wrap, and chill for at least 4 hours.

2. Combine the remaining ³⁄₄ cup confectioners' sugar and the strawberries in a large skillet over medium-high heat; cook until the strawberries just begin to soften, about 7 minutes. Transfer the berries to a medium bowl, cover with plastic wrap, and set aside for 45 minutes.

3. Strain the berry juice into the skillet and simmer over high heat until it thickens and reduces to about ³⁄₄ cup. Combine the strawberries, lemon juice, cornstarch, and reduced syrup in a large bowl, fold in the raspberries, and set the mixture aside. Place the brown sugar, with the remaining butter, hazelnuts, and flour, in a food processor and pulse just to combine. Set aside.

4. Preheat the oven to 400°F. On a lightly floured surface, between two sheets of waxed paper, roll the dough into a round at least 12 inches in diameter and about ¹⁄₁₆-inch thick; transfer the dough to a pie plate. Line the shell with parchment paper and fill it with dried beans or pie weights. Bake the shell until lightly browned, about 15 minutes. Remove the paper and beans; bake for 10 minutes longer. Transfer to a wire rack to cool completely.

5. Fill the pie shell with the berry mixture and top with the hazelnut crumble. Cover the edges of the crust with strips of foil, place the pie on a baking sheet, and bake until the filling bubbles, about 40 minutes. Transfer to a wire rack to cool completely.

Cherry-Berry Lattice Pie

Since sweet cherries have a short season, they are a hallmark of summer.
Here, we toss them with blueberries and encase the filling in a flaky latticework crust.

MAKES ONE 10-INCH PIE

2½ cups all-purpose flour

½ teaspoon salt

½ cup (1 stick) unsalted butter, chilled and cut into 2-inch pieces

½ cup vegetable shortening, chilled and cut into 1-inch pieces

⅓ cup ice water

4 cups (2 pints) fresh blueberries, stems removed

2 cups fresh sweet cherries, pitted

¾ cup sugar

3 tablespoons quick-cooking tapioca

1. In a large bowl, combine the flour and salt. Using a pastry blender or large fork, cut in the butter until pea-size pieces remain. Add the shortening and cut in until the mixture resembles coarse crumbs. Gradually add the water, 1 tablespoon at a time, tossing with the fork until combined. Gather the dough together and divide in half. Flatten each ball into a 6-inch disk; wrap in plastic wrap, and refrigerate at least 1 hour.

2. In a clean large bowl, combine the blueberries, cherries, sugar, and tapioca. Mix well and let the filling stand for 15 minutes. Preheat the oven to 400°F.

3. On a lightly floured surface, roll a piece of dough into an 11½-inch round; fit into a 10-inch pie pan. Roll the remaining dough into a round of the same size; cut into 12 strips, each about ¾-inch wide. Fill the pie pan with the fruit mixture. Weave the strips into a lattice pattern over the fruit (see page 16). Trim the edges and pinch the top and bottom crusts together.

4. Bake the pie for 20 minutes, then reduce the heat to 375°F. Continue baking until the crust is golden and the filling is bubbly, 30 to 40 minutes longer. (If necessary, cover the edges of the crust with strips of foil to prevent overbrowning.) Transfer to a wire rack to cool completely.

Nectarine-
Blueberry Pie

This beautiful pie is filled with the tastes of summer.
You'll feel like the ultimate host when you serve it at a picnic or barbecue.

MAKES ONE 9-INCH PIE

½ **recipe (2 disks) Grandma's Pie Dough (page 25)**

3½ **pounds nectarines, halved, pitted, and sliced ½-inch thick**

¾ **cup fresh blueberries, stems removed**

¾ **cup plus 1 tablespoon sugar**

3 **tablespoons quick-cooking tapioca, ground in a coffee mill or spice grinder**

2 **tablespoons fresh lemon juice**

1 **teaspoon finely grated lemon zest**

1 **large egg**

1 **tablespoon whole milk**

1. Preheat the oven to 450°F. On a lightly floured surface, roll the disks of dough into rounds about ⅛-inch thick; transfer one to a 9-inch pie pan. Place the remaining round on a baking sheet lined with parchment paper; chill both.

2. In a large bowl, toss together the nectarines, blueberries, ¾ cup sugar, tapioca, lemon juice, and zest. Set aside for 15 minutes, then drain through a fine-meshed sieve. In a small bowl, beat together the egg and milk; set aside.

3. Fill the prepared bottom crust with the fruit mixture and top it with the second dough round. Seal and flute the edges; brush the top with some of the prepared egg wash.

4. Cut a few slits in the top crust. Bake the pie for 10 minutes, then reduce the oven temperature to 425°F. Continue baking the pie for 25 minutes, then brush it with the remaining egg wash, sprinkle it with the remaining 1 tablespoon sugar, and continue to bake until golden brown, about 5 minutes longer. Cool on a wire rack.

Cranberry-Cherry Cobbler Pie

With this delicious dessert, you'll never have to choose between a cobbler and a pie again. Cranberries and cherries marry beautifully for a sweet-tart finish that is truly the best of both worlds!

MAKES ONE 9-INCH PIE

¼ cup cornstarch

1 teaspoon finely grated lime zest, plus 1 tablespoon lime juice, divided

⅔ cup plus 2 tablespoons sugar, plus more for sprinkling

1 teaspoon kosher salt, divided

12 ounces cranberries

12 ounces frozen sweet cherries

1½ cups all-purpose flour, spooned and leveled

2 teaspoons baking powder

½ cup cold unsalted butter, cut up

¾ cup buttermilk or whole milk

1. Preheat oven to 350°F. Whisk together cornstarch, lime zest and juice, ⅔ cup sugar, and ½ teaspoon salt. Add cranberries and cherries; toss to combine. Transfer to a 9-inch pie plate.

2. Whisk together flour, baking powder, 2 tablespoons sugar, and ½ teaspoon salt. Cut in butter until mixture resembles coarse meal. Add buttermilk and gently mix to form a wet, shaggy dough. Dollop mounds of dough on top of fruit; sprinkle with sugar. Bake, on a baking sheet, until golden and bubbling, 50 to 55 minutes; cool slightly.

Quince Mince Pie

Mincemeat, quince, and Granny Smith apples make this pie as delightfully golden as the childhood memories we associate with it. For a decorative flourish, finish with ornamental cutouts instead of a top crust. To save time, this recipe calls for store-bought pie dough.

MAKES ONE 9-INCH PIE

1 tablespoon finely chopped crystallized ginger

1 tablespoon sugar

2 cups store-bought mincemeat filling

¼ cup brandy

2 Granny Smith apples, peeled and finely chopped

2 quinces, peeled and finely chopped

1 cup chopped walnuts

1 cup golden raisins

Juice and zest of 2 oranges

Juice and zest of 1 lemon

2 (9-inch) store-bought unroll-and-fill piecrusts

2 teaspoons water

1 large egg, beaten

1. In a small food processor, combine the crystallized ginger and sugar. Process until the mixture is finely chopped; set aside. Place the mincemeat, brandy, apples, quinces, walnuts, raisins, and orange zest and juice in a large saucepan and bring to a simmer. Continue to cook over medium-low heat, covered, until the fruit is tender, about 30 minutes. Stir in the lemon zest and juice. Let the filling cool to room temperature. Preheat the oven to 375°F.

2. Fit one of the dough rounds into a 9-inch pie pan. Pour in the filling. Use small decorative cookie cutters to make cutout patterns in the remaining dough round; set the cutouts aside. Place the round carefully over the pie, taking care not to stretch the holes out of shape, and crimp the edges to seal. Add the water to the egg to make a wash, and brush it over the surface and edges of the crust. Sprinkle the pie with some of the reserved ginger-sugar mixture.

3. Transfer the reserved cutout crust pieces to a cookie sheet, brush them with the egg wash, and sprinkle them with the remaining ginger sugar. Bake the cutouts until they are just golden, about 12 minutes. Set them on a wire rack to cool.

4. Bake the pie until the top is golden and the filling is bubbling, 35 to 45 minutes. Decorate the pie with the cutout pastry pieces. Transfer to a wire rack to cool. Serve warm.

Apple-Raspberry Pie

This beautiful lattice pie brings together rich summer berries and crisp fall fruit.
Try adding a teaspoon of orange zest for an extra burst of fresh flavor.

2 tablespoons all-purpose flour, plus more for surface

Basic Pie Dough (page 25)

1/4 cup raspberry jam

2 tablespoons granulated sugar

1 teaspoon pure vanilla extract

1/4 teaspoon kosher salt

2 1/2 pounds Granny Smith, Golden Delicious, or Pink Lady apples, peeled and thinly sliced

1 cup frozen raspberries

Egg wash, for brushing crust

Raw sugar, for sprinkling

1. Preheat oven to 350°F. On a floured surface, roll one disk of dough to a 13-inch circle. Transfer to a 9-inch pie plate; trim overhang to 1 inch.

2. Whisk together flour, jam, granulated sugar, vanilla, and salt. Add apples and raspberries; toss to coat. Transfer to pie plate. Freeze 15 minutes.

3. On a floured surface, roll remaining disk of dough to a 13-inch circle. Cut into 1 1/2-inch strips; discard trimmings. Weave strips into a lattice pattern over fruit. Fold bottom overhang over lattice edges and crimp to seal. Brush dough with egg wash; sprinkle with raw sugar. Freeze 15 minutes.

4. Bake on a baking sheet until golden and bubbling, 60 to 75 minutes. Cool on a rack, at least 4 hours.

Pear Tartlets
with Brown-Sugar Crème Fraîche

Each tiny pastry shell cradles half a Bartlett pear dressed in an indulgent buttery glaze.
Drizzle the brown-sugar crème fraîche over top for a sinfully sweet finish.

MAKES 6 TARTLETS

1³/₄ cups all-purpose flour

¹/₂ cup granulated sugar

Salt

9 tablespoons unsalted butter, cold and cut into small pieces; plus 4¹/₂ tablespoons, at room temperature

3 Bartlett or Anjou pears, peeled, halved, and cored

¹/₂ cup crème fraîche

2 tablespoons light brown sugar

1. In a medium bowl, combine flour, 1¹/₂ tablespoons granulated sugar, and a heaping ¹/₄ teaspoon salt. Using your fingers, blend cold butter into mixture until mixture resembles coarse meal. Add 4 to 5 tablespoons ice water, adding more by the teaspoon if needed, until mixture forms a dough when pressed together. Pat dough into a disk, wrap tightly in plastic wrap, and refrigerate until chilled, about 30 minutes.

2. Preheat oven to 400°F. Meanwhile, place six 3¹/₂- to 4-inch ramekins on a baking pan. Add 1 tablespoon granulated sugar and ¹/₂ tablespoon room-temperature butter to each. Place a halved pear, cut-side up, in each ramekin. Bake for 25 minutes.

3. Meanwhile, on a lightly floured surface, roll out dough. Cut out 6 circles the same diameter as ramekins. Transfer dough circles to a plate, cover with plastic wrap, and refrigerate until pears are ready.

4. Remove pears from oven and, working quickly, place dough circles directly on top of pears to cover. Dot dough circles with remaining butter, then sprinkle each with ¹/₄ teaspoon granulated sugar. Bake until crust is golden and flaky, 15 to 20 minutes.

5. Let tartlets rest 3 to 4 minutes, then invert onto plates. Meanwhile, in a small bowl, combine crème fraîche and brown sugar. Serve tartlets warm with brown-sugar crème fraîche on the side.

Strawberry-Rhubarb Pie

Rhubarb and strawberries are a classic combination.
Encased in a golden-brown pie crust, the pairing becomes divine.

MAKES ONE 9-INCH PIE

½ **recipe (2 disks) Grandma's Pie Dough (page 25)**

1⅓ **pounds rhubarb, trimmed and cut into 1-inch pieces (see Tip)**

⅓ **pound strawberries, hulled and halved**

¾ **cup sugar**

⅓ **cup all-purpose flour**

1. Preheat the oven to 375°F and position the rack in the center. On a lightly floured surface, roll a disk of dough into a ⅛-inch-thick round and transfer to a 9-inch pie pan. Set aside and keep chilled. Roll the remaining dough to ⅛-inch thick. If you like, use a miniature star cutter (or other small shape) to create decorative vents in the top crust.

2. Combine the rhubarb, strawberries, sugar, and flour in a large bowl; transfer to the prepared pie pan. Drape the rolled-out dough over the pie, taking care not to stretch the decorative vents out of shape. (If you did not cut decorative holes in the top crust, use a sharp paring knife to cut slits in it now.) Trim the edges of both crusts, leaving a ½-inch overhang. Fold the dough under and lightly pinch to seal the top and bottom crusts. Crimp around the rim and chill for 10 minutes.

3. Bake until the crust is golden brown and the filling is bubbling, 45 to 55 minutes. Transfer to a wire rack to cool completely.

TIP

If you can't find fresh rhubarb, use frozen. You'll find it in the grocer's freezer section.

Custard
& Cream
Pies

Meyer-Lemon Tart
with Gingersnap Crust and Almond Whipped Cream

This bright, sunny tart combines the tang of lemon with the spice of gingersnaps and the nuttiness of almonds. Try using one of our crumb crusts (page 26) for a slightly sweeter variation.

MAKES ONE 9-INCH TART

2 cups crushed gingersnaps

¼ cup dark-brown sugar

4 tablespoons unsalted butter, melted and cooled, plus 6 more tablespoons, cut into small pieces

2 large eggs, plus 3 large egg yolks

¼ cup granulated sugar

½ teaspoon cornstarch

⅓ cup fresh Meyer lemon juice (from about 3 lemons)

3 tablespoons Meyer lemon zest

1 vanilla bean, seeds scraped and reserved

1 cup heavy cream

1 tablespoon confectioners' sugar

¼ teaspoon almond extract

1. Preheat oven to 350°F. Meanwhile, in a medium bowl, mix crushed cookies, brown sugar, and cooled melted butter with a spoon until combined. In a 9-inch fluted tart pan with a removable bottom, press cookie mixture in an even layer on the bottom and up the sides. Bake until fragrant, 10 minutes. Remove from oven and transfer pan to a wire rack to cool.

2. Increase oven temperature to 375°F. In a medium saucepan, off heat, whisk eggs and yolks, granulated sugar, and cornstarch until combined. Transfer saucepan to medium-low heat. Add lemon juice and zest, and whisk continuously until mixture is thick enough to coat the back of a wooden spoon, 6 to 8 minutes. Remove from heat and whisk in butter pieces and vanilla seeds.

3. Pour mixture into cooled cookie shell. Transfer to oven and bake until crust darkens slightly, 20 minutes. Transfer to a wire rack and let tart cool to room temperature.

4. In a medium bowl, using an electric mixer on high speed, whip cream until soft peaks form, 3 minutes. Add confectioners' sugar and almond extract, and whip until the peaks are almost stiff, about 2 minutes more. Slice tart and serve each slice with a dollop of almond whipped cream.

Mississippi Mud Pie

The Crown Restaurant in Indianola, Mississippi, created this mud pie with a layer of chocolate custard, vanilla ice cream, and a drizzle of rich fudge sauce. Here, we use a store-bought piecrust for ease. (You can also use the Baked Pie Shell on page 24 and skip step 1.) According to folklore, the Delta region's beloved chocolate pie was so named because its fudgy base resembles the muddy bottom of the Mississippi River.

MAKES ONE 9-INCH PIE

1 (9-inch) store-bought piecrust

½ cup (1 stick) unsalted butter, softened

1¾ cups sugar

¼ cup cocoa

¼ cup all-purpose flour

4 large eggs, beaten

1 teaspoon pure vanilla extract

3 cups vanilla or mocha ice cream, slightly softened

3 tablespoons fudge sauce

1. Preheat the oven to 450°F. Line the unbaked crust with parchment paper and fill it with dried beans or pie weights; bake until the dough is lightly golden and set, 10 to 15 minutes. Cool the crust on a wire rack. Reduce the oven temperature to 350°F.

2. In a bowl, stir together the butter, sugar, and cocoa until well combined. Add the flour, eggs, and vanilla and mix until smooth. Pour the filling into the prepared crust and bake for 30 to 40 minutes.

3. Transfer to a wire rack to cool completely. Gently mound ice cream over the pie and freeze until the ice cream sets. Drizzle with fudge sauce before serving.

Lemon Meringue Pie

This classic dessert has delighted American families since the early 1800s. For voluminous meringue, bring the egg whites to room temperature before whipping them, and make certain your whisk and bowl are very clean. The dough contains vegetable shortening for an extra-flaky crust.

MAKES ONE 9-INCH PIE

2¼ cups all-purpose flour

1¼ cups plus 7 tablespoons sugar

¼ teaspoon salt

15 tablespoons unsalted butter, chilled and cut into small pieces

¼ cup vegetable shortening, chilled

4 to 6 tablespoons ice water

5 tablespoons cornstarch

1½ cups water

½ cup fresh lemon juice (from about 3 lemons)

1 tablespoon finely grated lemon zest

3 large eggs, separated

1. Combine the flour, 2 tablespoons sugar, and salt in a large bowl. Cut in 12 tablespoons butter and the shortening using a pastry blender, 2 knives, or your fingers until the mixture resembles coarse meal. Stir in the ice water, 1 tablespoon at a time, until the dough just holds together when pressed. Transfer the dough to a lightly floured work surface, gather it together, and flatten it into a disk. Wrap the dough in plastic wrap and chill for at least 1 hour or up to overnight. (The chilled dough may be frozen for up to 3 months.)

2. Preheat the oven to 425°F. On a lightly floured surface, roll the dough into a ⅛-inch-thick circle and fit it gently into a 9-inch pie pan. Trim away the excess dough, leaving a ½-inch overhang. Fold the edges under and crimp them along the rim. Prick the bottom of the dough several times with a fork, line with parchment paper, and fill with beans or pie weights. Bake for 15 minutes. Remove the paper and weights and bake for 15 minutes more. Transfer to a wire rack to cool completely. Reduce the oven temperature to 350°F.

3. Meanwhile, whisk the cornstarch, 1¼ cups sugar, and water together in a medium saucepan. Add the lemon juice, zest, and egg yolks; cook the mixture over medium heat, stirring constantly, until it begins to bubble and thicken, about 10 minutes. Remove the lemon curd from the heat, whisk in the remaining 3 tablespoons butter, and pour it through a strainer into the prepared crust.

4. Beat the egg whites to soft peaks. Add the remaining 5 tablespoons sugar in a slow, steady stream, and continue to beat until the whites have increased about six times in volume and are glossy and firm. (They will make pointy peaks when the beaters or whisk are lifted.)

5. Spread the meringue over the filling, taking care to spread the edges of the crust all around. Bake until the meringue is golden brown, 10 to 15 minutes. Transfer to a wire rack to cool completely.

Mocha Cream Pie

It's a chocolate-lover's dream: a crunchy chocolate cookie crust filled with a rich and creamy chocolate-coffee filling, topped with homemade whipped cream and chocolate shavings.

MAKES ONE 9-INCH PIE

40 chocolate wafer cookies

¾ cup sugar, divided

¾ teaspoon kosher salt, divided

4 tablespoons unsalted butter, melted

½ cup semisweet chocolate chips

¼ cup cornstarch

4 large egg yolks

2 cups half-and-half

½ cup brewed coffee

1 cup heavy cream

Shaved chocolate, for serving

1. Preheat oven to 350°F. Process cookies, 2 tablespoons sugar, and ½ teaspoon salt in a food processor until fine crumbs form, 15 to 30 seconds. Add butter and pulse to combine, 5 to 10 times. Press cookie mixture into the bottom and up the sides of a 9-inch pie plate. Bake, on a baking sheet, until crust is dry and set, 18 to 20 minutes. Cool on a rack.

2. Place chocolate chips in a bowl. Whisk together cornstarch, egg yolks, ½ cup sugar, and ¼ teaspoon salt in a medium saucepan. Whisk in half-and-half and coffee. Cook over medium-low heat, whisking constantly, until thickened and the whisk holds a trail, 6 to 8 minutes. Strain over chocolate chips. Let stand 2 minutes; whisk until smooth.

3. Transfer pudding to cooled crust and smooth the top. Press plastic wrap directly on surface of pudding to prevent a skin from forming. Chill, at least 4 hours.

4. Discard plastic wrap. Whip cream and 2 tablespoons sugar to medium peaks and dollop over chilled pie.

5. Serve topped with shaved chocolate.

Rhubarb Custard Pie with Pecan Crust

Celebrate the first spring rhubarb with this simple, luscious pie.
The nutty crust contrasts nicely with the creamy filling.

MAKES ONE 9-INCH PIE

CRUST

½ cup pecan halves

1⅓ cups all-purpose flour

½ cup sugar

½ cup (1 stick) unsalted butter, chilled and cut into pieces

2 large egg yolks

1 tablespoon pure vanilla extract

1 large egg white

1 teaspoon water

FILLING

1¼ pounds rhubarb, trimmed and coarsely chopped (4 cups)

⅔ cup sugar

1 teaspoon grated lemon zest

¼ teaspoon salt

2 large eggs

1 large egg yolk

1¼ cups heavy cream

1 tablespoon cornstarch

1. **Make the crust:** Preheat the oven to 400°F. In a food processor fitted with a metal blade, process the pecans until finely ground. Add the flour and sugar; process until combined. Add the butter, egg yolks, and vanilla; process until the mixture resembles coarse crumbs.

2. Press the crumb mixture into the bottom and up the sides of a 9-inch pie pan; crimp decoratively along the edge. With the tines of a fork, prick the bottom and sides of the crust. In a small bowl, mix together the egg white and water. Brush the bottom and sides of the crust with the egg wash. Bake until golden brown, 10 to 12 minutes. Transfer to a wire rack to cool completely. Reduce the oven temperature to 350°F.

3. **Make the filling:** In a large bowl, combine the rhubarb, sugar, lemon zest, and salt. Spoon the filling into the crust. In a medium bowl, beat together the eggs and egg yolk. Mix in the cream and cornstarch. Spoon over the rhubarb mixture.

4. **Finish the pie:** Cover the edge of the crust with foil to prevent overbrowning and bake the pie until the custard is firm, 25 to 30 minutes. Transfer to a wire rack to cool completely.

Orange Meringue Pie

This old-fashioned pie makes a great gift. Present it inside a vintage tin
lined with waxed paper or tissue paper.

MAKES ONE 9-INCH PIE

2 cups sugar

3 tablespoons all-purpose flour

3½ tablespoons cornstarch

¼ teaspoon salt

½ cup orange juice concentrate

3 tablespoons fresh lemon juice

1½ cups water

2 tablespoons unsalted butter

4 eggs, separated

1 Baked Pie Shell (page 24)

1 teaspoon pure vanilla extract

½ teaspoon cream of tartar

1. Whisk 1½ cups sugar together with the flour, cornstarch, and salt in a large saucepan. Add the juice concentrate, lemon juice, and water. Bring the mixture to a boil, whisking continuously. Whisk in the butter and remove the pan from the heat.

2. Lightly beat the egg yolks in a medium bowl. Drizzle in ½ cup hot juice mixture while whisking the yolks, then slowly add the yolk mixture to the juice mixture in the saucepan. Cook over medium-low heat until the filling is very thick and glossy, about 5 minutes. Pour it through a strainer into the prepared pie shell and set aside.

3. Preheat the oven to 350°F. Beat the egg whites, vanilla, and cream of tartar to soft peaks using a handheld mixer set on medium speed. Increase the mixer speed to high, gradually add the remaining ½ cup sugar, and continue to beat until stiff peaks form. Gently spread the meringue over the hot filling, taking care to spread it all around to the edges of the crust (see Tip). Use a spoon to make a pattern of dips and peaks on the surface of the meringue. Bake until the meringue is lightly browned, about 10 minutes. Transfer to a wire rack to cool completely.

> ### TIP
>
> To prevent the meringue topping from shrinking, make sure it touches the crust. It will "grab" the edges while it browns.

Key Lime Tart

Louie's Backyard in Key West, Florida, bakes up this creamy variation on Key lime pie. Instead of the familiar graham-cracker crust, they use a ginger-molasses pastry that contrasts beautifully with the zestiness of the limes.

MAKES ONE 11-INCH TART

CRUST

¹⁄₃ cup sugar

¹⁄₂ cup (1 stick) unsalted butter, at room temperature

Pinch salt

1¹⁄₂ cups plus 2 tablespoons all-purpose flour

1 large egg

¹⁄₂ teaspoon pure vanilla extract

2 tablespoons molasses

¹⁄₂ tablespoon ground ginger

¹⁄₄ teaspoon ground cinnamon

FILLING

1 (14-ounce) can sweetened condensed milk

¹⁄₂ cup Key lime juice

4 large egg yolks

1 tablespoon vanilla extract

1. **For the crust:** Preheat the oven to 325°F. In a medium bowl, cream the sugar, butter, and salt until smooth. Add the flour, egg, vanilla, molasses, ginger, and cinnamon; mix well to form a smooth dough. On a lightly floured surface, roll the dough into a 13-inch round about ¹⁄₄-inch thick. Gently press the dough into an 11-inch tart pan with a removable bottom. Trim the excess around the rim. Bake until browned, 12 to 15 minutes.

2. **Assemble the tart:** In a medium bowl, whisk together all the filling ingredients. Pour the mixture into the prepared shell and bake until the filling sets to the consistency of a soft custard, about 15 minutes. Transfer to a wire rack to cool completely.

Pumpkin Cream Tartlets with Gingersnap Crust

With our easy gingersnap cookie crust, there's no fuss or muss. You simply mix the cookie crumbs and butter in a bowl, then pat the mixture into tartlet pans. Finish with the sweet-tart cranberry topping for a holiday-worthy presentation.

MAKES 8 TARTLETS

CRUST

3 cups gingersnap crumbs (about 50 cookies)

2 teaspoons ground cinnamon

3/4 cup (1 1/2 sticks) unsalted butter, melted

CRANBERRY TOPPING

2 cups sugar

1/2 cup water

1 cup fresh raspberries

PUMPKIN CREAM FILLING

1/2 cup whole milk

1 teaspoon unflavored gelatin

1 cup pumpkin puree

3/4 cup sugar

2 teaspoons brandy or cognac

4 teaspoons ground cinnamon

1/4 teaspoon ground nutmeg

1/4 teaspoon ground cloves

4 large egg yolks

1 cup heavy cream, whipped to stiff peaks

1. **Make the crusts:** Preheat the oven to 350°F. In a large bowl, combine the crumbs, cinnamon, and butter. Press the crumb mixture into the bottom and up the sides of eight 3 1/2-inch tartlet pans with removable bottoms. Place the tartlet shells on a baking sheet and bake for 10 minutes. Transfer them to a wire rack to cool completely.

2. **Make the cranberry topping:** In a small saucepan, bring the sugar and water to a boil over high heat. Add the cranberries and cook until they just begin to soften. With a slotted spoon, transfer the cranberries to a small bowl and set aside. Reserve the cranberry syrup for another use.

3. **Make the filling:** Fill a large bowl with ice and water; set aside. Place the milk in a small bowl, sprinkle the gelatin over it, and set aside. In a large saucepan, combine the pumpkin puree, sugar, brandy, cinnamon, nutmeg, cloves, and egg yolks. Cook the pumpkin mixture over medium heat, whisking constantly, until it begins to bubble and the temperature registers 140°F on an instant-read thermometer. Stir in the milk mixture and cook 1 minute more; transfer the custard to a medium bowl and set it over the prepared ice bath, stirring occasionally, until cool, about 10 minutes. Fold the whipped cream into the chilled pumpkin custard.

4. Divide the filling among the cooled crusts and smooth the tops. Chill for 6 hours or overnight.

5. Top each tartlet with a spoonful of candied cranberries, and serve cold.

Chocolate-Caramel Cream Pie

Chocoholics everywhere will adore this rich pie, which boasts a chocolate filling and a chocolate wafer crust. Top with homemade caramel sauce, or use your favorite store-bought brand.

MAKES ONE 9-INCH PIE

1/2 cup (1 stick) unsalted butter

2 cups finely crushed chocolate wafer cookies (about 36 cookies)

2 tablespoons cognac

5 ounces bittersweet chocolate, finely chopped

4 large egg yolks

2/3 cup plus 2 tablespoons dark brown sugar

1 tablespoon cornstarch

1/8 teaspoon salt

2 cups plus 2 tablespoons heavy cream

1 cup plus 2 tablespoons whole milk

1 1/2 teaspoons pure vanilla extract

Caramel Sauce (recipe below)

1 tablespoon cocoa powder

1. Preheat the oven to 350°F. Melt 4 tablespoons butter; combine it with the cookie crumbs and cognac in a medium bowl. Press the crumb mixture into the bottom and up the sides of a 9-inch pie pan. Bake for 10 minutes, and then cool completely on a wire rack.

2. Place the chocolate in a large bowl and set aside. Whisk the egg yolks, 2/3 cup brown sugar, cornstarch, and salt in a medium bowl; set aside. Heat the milk, 1/2 cup plus 2 tablespoons of the cream, and the remaining 4 tablespoons butter in a medium saucepan over medium-high heat, until the mixture just begins to boil. Whisking constantly, gradually pour the hot milk into the egg mixture. Return the custard to the saucepan and, whisking constantly, cook over medium heat until it comes to a boil. Cook for 1 minute more, still whisking, and stir in 1 teaspoon vanilla. Strain the pudding into the bowl with the chocolate. Let sit for 2 minutes, allowing the chocolate to melt, and then use a rubber spatula to fold the mixture together. Cool to room temperature.

3. Pour the caramel sauce into the piecrust; refrigerate for 10 minutes. Spread the pudding over the caramel and chill for 2 hours. Beat the remaining 1 1/2 cups cream, 2 tablespoons brown sugar, and 1/2 teaspoon vanilla with the cocoa powder in a large bowl until stiff peaks form. Spread over the pudding and chill for 30 minutes or up to 6 hours before serving.

CARAMEL SAUCE

3/4 cup sugar	1/4 cup heavy cream
1/4 cup water	1 tablespoon unsalted butter

Combine the sugar and water in a small saucepan over medium heat, stirring occasionally until the sugar dissolves. Increase the temperature to high and cook until the caramel turns an amber color. Remove the pan from the heat and stir in the cream, 1/8 cup at a time, until smooth. Add the butter and stir until melted. Cool until the sauce has thickened slightly, then use immediately or refrigerate in a microwaveable container for up to 3 weeks. To reheat, microwave on high for 1 to 2 minutes, stirring twice.

Orange-Buttermilk Chess Pie

Simple flavors take center stage in this take on a Southern staple, inspired by the winner at the 2013 State Fair of Texas. Garnished with beautiful candied orange slices, we've created a pie that looks as great as it tastes!

MAKES ONE 9-INCH PIE

Perfect Piecrust (page 22), unbaked

1½ cups sugar

3 tablespoons plain yellow cornmeal

¼ teaspoon salt

4 large eggs, lightly beaten

⅓ cup buttermilk

1½ teaspoons vanilla extract

1½ teaspoons orange zest

2 tablespoons fresh orange juice

2 tablespoons melted butter, cooled slightly

CANDIED ORANGE SLICES

1¼ cups sugar

1¼ cups water

2 small navel oranges, thinly sliced

1. Roll out half the dough (one disk) on a lightly floured sheet of parchment paper to ¼-inch thickness (about a 12-inch circle). Fit into a 9-inch pie plate, crimping edges as desired. Refrigerate 30 minutes to 1 hour.

2. Preheat oven to 325°F.

3. Whisk together sugar, cornmeal, and salt in a medium mixing bowl. Whisk together eggs, buttermilk, and next 4 ingredients in another medium mixing bowl. Add egg mixture to dry ingredients, stirring until well combined. Pour mixture into prepared crust.

4. Bake at 325°F for 45 to 50 minutes, or just until filling is set and center jiggles slightly when gently shaken.

5. Cool completely on a wire rack. Top with candied orange slices.

6. **For candied orange slices:** Bring sugar and water to a boil in a large saucepan over medium heat. Add orange slices and reduce heat to low. Simmer, flipping occasionally, until oranges are translucent but hold their shape, about 30 minutes.

7. Set a wire rack over a baking sheet. Gently transfer oranges onto rack in a single layer. Let stand until dry and slightly firm, about 8 hours.

TIP

The leftover candied-orange liquid is great to sweeten iced tea.

Butterscotch Pie

Your friends and family will adore this sweet custard pie. Dress it up with a sprinkle of toasted nuts or grated chocolate. For a winning wedge, always slice cream or custard pies when they are well-chilled.

MAKES ONE 9-INCH PIE

½ cup (1 stick) unsalted butter

1¼ cups light brown sugar

1½ cups hot water

¼ cup cornstarch

3 tablespoons all-purpose flour

½ teaspoon salt

1½ cups heavy cream

½ cup whole milk

4 egg yolks

1 teaspoon pure vanilla extract

1 Baked Pie Shell (page 24)

1 teaspoon honey

2 tablespoons confectioners' sugar

¼ cup toasted almond slices (optional)

1. Melt the butter in a medium saucepan over medium heat until it begins to brown. Stir in the brown sugar. Add the hot water and whisk until the mixture comes to a boil. Continue to cook for 2 minutes more; remove the pan from the heat and set aside.

2. Combine the cornstarch, flour, and salt in a small bowl. Whisk in ½ cup cream and the milk until smooth; pour into the butter mixture. Whisk continuously over medium heat until the mixture comes to a boil and thickens, about 3 minutes. Remove the pan from the heat. Lightly beat the egg yolks in a medium bowl. Stream in ½ cup of the hot mixture while whisking the yolks. Whisk the egg mixture into the milk mixture in the saucepan, and cook over medium heat for 1 minute. Pour the custard through a strainer and into a bowl; stir in the vanilla. Pour the custard into the prepared pie shell and chill until set.

3. Beat the remaining 1 cup cream with the honey and confectioners' sugar until stiff peaks form. Spread the cream over the cooled pie and chill. Sprinkle with toasted almonds, if desired, before serving.

S'mores Galette

Who wouldn't love s'mores in pie form? You get all the delicious flavors
of the childhood classic, minus the bonfire and sticky fingers!

MAKES ONE 11-INCH GALETTE

3 tablespoons all-purpose flour,
plus more for surface

$1/2$ **recipe (1 disk) Basic Pie
Dough (page 25)**

2 graham crackers, divided

$2/3$ **cup sugar**

$1/3$ **cup cocoa powder**

$1/4$ **teaspoon kosher salt**

4 tablespoons unsalted butter,
melted

$1/2$ **teaspoon pure vanilla extract**

1 large egg, plus egg wash
for crust

6 large marshmallows, halved

1. Preheat oven to 350°F. On a floured surface, roll pie dough to a 13-inch
circle. Transfer to a baking sheet and crumble 1$1/2$ graham crackers over
dough, leaving a 2-inch border. Refrigerate for 15 minutes.

2. Whisk together sugar, cocoa powder, and salt. Whisk in butter. Whisk in
vanilla and egg. Spread batter over dough and graham crackers, leaving a
2-inch border. Fold dough over batter; brush dough with egg wash.

3. Bake until golden and set, 20 to 25 minutes. Remove from oven and top
with marshmallows. Bake until marshmallows are golden, 5 to 10 minutes
more. Crush remaining $1/2$ graham cracker and sprinkle over top; cool slightly
before serving.

Banana Pudding Pie

A retro dessert is turned into an irresistible pie featuring fresh bananas,
a crust made from vanilla wafers, and loads of gooey caramel.

MAKES ONE 9-INCH PIE

1 recipe Vanilla-Wafer Crumb Crust (page 26), prebaked

3 egg yolks

2 tablespoons cornstarch

1/2 cup granulated sugar

1/4 teaspoon salt

1 teaspoon powdered gelatin

1 cup whole milk, chilled

1 cup heavy cream

1 vanilla bean, pod and scraped seeds

1 1/2 teaspoons unsalted butter

3/4 teaspoon pure vanilla extract

1 cup fresh whipped cream

5 tablespoons caramel sauce, store-bought or homemade (page 78), plus extra for garnish

3 medium bananas, sliced

1. Place a medium bowl inside a larger bowl filled with ice water; set aside. In another bowl, whisk the egg yolks, cornstarch, sugar, and salt together until very thick and light in color; set aside. Sprinkle gelatin over 1/4 cup of the cold milk; let sit for 5 minutes.

2. In a medium pot, bring the cream, remaining 3/4 cup milk, and vanilla bean and seeds to a boil. Slowly whisk the warm cream mixture into the egg mixture, pour the custard back into the pot, and cook over medium-low heat, stirring, until it reaches a boil. Pour the custard through a fine-mesh strainer into the prepared chilled bowl; stir in the gelatin mixture, butter, and vanilla extract. Let cool; fold in whipped cream to create the pudding.

3. Spread caramel sauce over the prepared crust, reserving 1 tablespoon to drizzle on top of pie. Line the crust with slices from 2 1/2 bananas and top with the pudding. Chill for 2 hours. Decorate the pie with the remaining banana slices and caramel.

Nut Pies

Pumpkin-Pecan Pie

Why not serve two favorites in a single pie? Guests will be surprised to find a creamy pumpkin filling beneath what appears to be a traditional pecan pie. Be forewarned: This pie is so rich, small slices will satisfy even the most ardent dessert enthusiasts.

MAKES TWO 9-INCH PIES

CRUST

2 cups all-purpose flour, unsifted

³/₄ cup (1¹/₂ sticks) unsalted butter, chilled

6 to 7 tablespoons ice water

PUMPKIN LAYER

2 large eggs, separated

¹/₂ cup sugar

1 (16-ounce) can pumpkin, or 2 cups well-drained fresh pumpkin puree

¹/₂ cup half-and-half

2 teaspoons pumpkin pie spice

¹/₂ teaspoon salt

PECAN LAYER

3 tablespoons unsalted butter

¹/₂ cup sugar

1 cup dark corn syrup

1 teaspoon pure vanilla extract

2 large eggs

2 cups pecan halves

1. **For the crust:** Put the flour in a large bowl. Cut in the butter using a pastry blender, 2 knives, or your fingers until the mixture resembles coarse meal. Sprinkle in the ice water, 1 tablespoon at a time, tossing lightly after each addition, just until the pastry holds together. Divide the dough in half and shape each piece into a disk. Wrap each disk in plastic wrap and refrigerate for at least 1 hour.

2. On a lightly floured surface, roll one disk into a 12-inch round. Gently fit the dough into a 9-inch pie pan, fold the overhang inward, and form a high fluted edge. Repeat with the other pastry disk; refrigerate while you prepare the pumpkin filling. Preheat the oven to 350°F.

3. **For the pumpkin layer:** In a small bowl, using a handheld mixer on high speed, beat the egg whites until soft peaks form. In a large bowl, with the same beaters and the mixer on low speed, beat the egg yolks, sugar, pumpkin, half-and-half, pumpkin pie spice, and salt until blended. With a rubber spatula, fold the egg whites into the pumpkin mixture. Divide the filling between the two pie shells and bake for 30 minutes.

4. **Meanwhile, prepare the pecan layer:** In a 1-quart saucepan over low heat, melt the butter. Remove the pan from the heat and stir in the sugar, corn syrup, and vanilla. Beat in the eggs.

5. Carefully arrange the pecans in a single layer on top of the pumpkin layer in a decorative pattern. Pour the sugar mixture over the pecans, taking care not to disturb them.

6. Return the pies to the oven and bake until a knife inserted 1 inch from the edge comes out clean, 15 to 20 minutes longer. Transfer to a wire rack to cool completely. Gently cover and chill.

Peach-Almond Galette

Fresh peaches are the star in this homey, feel-good dessert.
Touches of almond, honey, and cinnamon are sure to satisfy your sweet tooth.

MAKES ONE 10-INCH GALETTE

1½ cups all-purpose flour, plus more for dusting

½ cup yellow cornmeal

1 tablespoon granulated sugar, plus 2 teaspoons for sprinkling

½ teaspoon salt

10 tablespoons cold unsalted butter, cut into pieces

3 to 5 tablespoons ice water

½ cup whole almonds (about 2½ ounces)

½ cup confectioners' sugar

1 large egg yolk

1 teaspoon almond extract

8 peaches (about 2½ pounds), peeled and sliced

2 tablespoons honey

½ teaspoon cinnamon

1. In a food processor, combine flour, cornmeal, 1 tablespoon granulated sugar, and salt. Add butter; pulse until mixture resembles coarse meal. Add ice water, 1 tablespoon at a time, and pulse until a dough forms. Shape dough into a disk, wrap in plastic wrap, and refrigerate until chilled, about 30 minutes.

2. Meanwhile, in a clean food processor, grind almonds and confectioners' sugar to a fine meal. Add the egg yolk and almond extract and blend; set aside. In a large bowl, combine peaches, honey, and cinnamon; set aside.

3. Preheat oven to 400°F. On a lightly floured work surface, roll dough out to a 14-inch circle. Fit into a 10-inch pie plate. Spread almond paste over dough, including up the sides. Add peaches. Fold edges of dough over peaches to form a rustic flat pie with about a 2-inch-wide border. Brush dough with water and sprinkle with remaining granulated sugar. Bake until filling is bubbling and crust is flaky and golden brown, 45 to 50 minutes.

Brownie Pecan Tart

A gooey delicious brownie—comprised of bittersweet chocolate, brown sugar, vanilla, and unsweetened cocoa powder—gets a nutty makeover in this jazzy tart mash-up.

Basic Brownie Batter
(recipe below)

²/₃ cup chopped pecans

2 tablespoons unsalted butter, melted

¹/₂ cup packed light brown sugar

4 tablespoons dark Karo syrup

¹/₂ teaspoon vanilla extract

¹/₈ teaspoon salt

1. Preheat oven to 350°F. Spread Basic Brownie Batter into a buttered and floured 11-inch tart pan with a removable bottom.

2. Bake for 20 minutes. Meanwhile, in a large bowl, combine remaining ingredients. Remove tart from oven and spread pecan mixture over top. Continue baking until a skewer inserted into the center comes out with a few moist crumbs, about 15 minutes more. Let cool before releasing tart from pan.

BASIC BROWNIE BATTER

1 stick unsalted butter, plus more for pans

8 ounces bittersweet chocolate, chopped

³/₄ cup granulated sugar

¹/₂ cup packed light brown sugar

3 large eggs

1¹/₂ teaspoons vanilla extract

³/₄ teaspoon salt

¹/₂ cup all-purpose flour, plus more for pans

3 tablespoons unsweetened cocoa

In a heatproof bowl over a pot of simmering water, melt butter. Add chocolate and stir until melted. Remove bowl from heat and set aside. In a large bowl, lightly beat together sugars, eggs, vanilla, and salt until combined. Stir in reserved chocolate mixture. Add flour and cocoa and stir until just combined.

Chocolate-Coconut Pecan Pie

We've increased the wow-factor of a classic pecan pie by
adding chocolate and coconut to the mix. The result is deliciously exotic.

MAKES ONE 9-INCH PIE

All-purpose flour, for surface

½ **recipe (1 disk) Basic Pie Dough (page 25)**

2 cups pecans

½ **cup semisweet chocolate chips**

½ **cup unsweetened coconut flakes**

1 cup packed light brown sugar

1 cup light corn syrup

3 large eggs

4 tablespoons unsalted butter, melted

¼ teaspoon kosher salt

1. Preheat oven to 350°F. On a floured surface, roll dough to a 13-inch circle. Transfer to a 9-inch pie plate, fold edges under to align with the rim of the plate, and crimp.

2. Scatter pecans, chocolate chips, and coconut over bottom of the pie shell; place on a baking sheet. Whisk together sugar, corn syrup, eggs, butter, and salt; pour into shell.

3. Bake until filling is set, 50 to 60 minutes (tent with foil if coconut becomes too dark). Cool, on a rack, for at least 4 hours.

Salted Caramel Peanut Butter Fudge Pie

The salted caramel and peanut butter topping
on this pie make this a chocolate dessert no one will forget!

MAKES ONE 9-INCH PIE

½ **package refrigerated piecrusts**

1 **cup (2 sticks) butter**

½ **cup creamy peanut butter**

1¼ **cups firmly packed brown sugar**

1¼ **cups all-purpose flour**

½ **cup roasted unsalted peanuts**

3 **ounces unsweetened baking chocolate**

½ **cup granulated sugar**

2 **tablespoons unsweetened cocoa**

3 **large eggs**

2 **teaspoons vanilla extract**

¼ **teaspoon salt**

1 **jar caramel topping or** 1½ **cups homemade caramel sauce (page 78)**

½ **teaspoon flaked sea salt**

1. Heat oven to 350°F. Fit refrigerated piecrust into a 9-inch glass pie plate according to package directions; fold edges under and crimp as desired.

2. Using a fork, stir together ¼ cup softened butter, ¼ cup peanut butter, ¼ cup brown sugar, and ½ cup flour in a bowl until crumbly; stir in peanuts. Freeze for 15 minutes.

3. Meanwhile, microwave chocolate and remaining ¾ cup butter in a microwave-safe bowl on high, 1½ to 2 minutes or until melted and smooth, stirring at 30-second intervals. Whisk in granulated sugar, cocoa, and remaining 1 cup brown sugar. Add eggs, one at a time, whisking just until blended after each addition. Whisk in vanilla, salt, and remaining ¾ cup flour. Pour mixture into prepared piecrust. Crumble peanut butter mixture over top of pie. (The peanut butter mixture will extend above the rim but will not overflow when baked.)

4. Bake at 350°F for 50 to 55 minutes, or until center of pie is puffed and set. Remove from oven and cool on a wire rack for 20 minutes.

5. In a small bowl, stir together caramel topping and remaining ¼ cup peanut butter; drizzle 4 tablespoons over top of pie. Cool pie completely, about 1 hour. Sprinkle with flaked sea salt and serve with remaining sauce.

Pumpkin Pie with Oat-Pecan Crust

Looking for a twist on the traditional pumpkin pie? Pump up the crust
with candied pecans for a unique take on this holiday favorite.

MAKES ONE 9-INCH PIE

2 cups pecans

1 cup old-fashioned rolled oats

4 tablespoons unsalted butter,
melted

2 tablespoons granulated sugar

3/4 teaspoon kosher salt, divided

1 cup pure pumpkin puree

1/2 cup heavy cream

1/3 cup packed light brown sugar

1/4 cup whole milk

2 large eggs, plus 1 large egg
white

1/2 teaspoon ground cinnamon

1/2 teaspoon ground ginger

Pinch ground cloves

Candied pecans, for serving

1. Preheat oven to 350°F. Toast pecans and oats on a baking sheet until
golden and fragrant, 10 to 12 minutes; cool.

2. Process pecans, oats, butter, granulated sugar, and 1/2 teaspoon salt in a
food processor until finely ground, 2 to 4 minutes. Press mixture in bottom
and up sides of a 9-inch pie plate. Freeze for 15 minutes. Bake on a baking
sheet until set, 20 to 25 minutes. Cool on a rack.

3. Whisk together pumpkin, cream, brown sugar, milk, eggs, cinnamon,
ginger, cloves, and 1/4 teaspoon salt. Pour into crust and bake until filling is
set, 40 to 45 minutes. Cool on a rack. Chill at least 2 hours.

4. Serve topped with candied pecans.

Almond Cheesecake Tart

A sweet cheesecake filling is encased in a nutty graham-cracker crust
and topped with fresh raspberries and blueberries for the perfect summer treat.

GRAHAM-CRACKER CRUST

½ **cup slivered almonds**

1 **tablespoon sugar**

11 **graham crackers**

6 **tablespoons butter or margarine**

CHEESE FILLING

1½ **packages cream cheese**

½ **cup sugar**

2 **large eggs**

¼ **teaspoon vanilla extract**

¼ **teaspoon almond extract**

Raspberries and blueberries, for garnish

1. Preheat oven to 375°F.

2. **Prepare graham-cracker crust:** In food processor with knife blade attached, pulse almonds with sugar until finely ground; add graham crackers and pulse until fine crumbs form. Pour in melted butter; pulse until moistened. With hand, press mixture firmly onto bottom and up sides of 11-inch tart pan with removable bottom. Bake crust for 10 minutes. Cool on wire rack.

3. Reset oven control to 350°F.

4. **Prepare cheese filling:** In medium bowl, with mixer on low speed, beat cream cheese and sugar until smooth, occasionally scraping bowl with rubber spatula. Add eggs and extracts; beat just until combined.

5. Pour cheese mixture into cooled crust. Bake for 20 minutes or until set. Cool tart on wire rack. Cover and refrigerate at least 2 hours.

6. To serve, arrange berries decoratively on top of tart for garnish.

Blueberry-Almond Tart

Sweet summer blueberries and a buttery almond filling
are perfect partners in this heavenly tart!

MAKES ONE 11-INCH TART

CRUST

1½ cups all-purpose flour

½ teaspoon salt

½ cup butter or margarine

2 tablespoons vegetable shortening

5 tablespoons cold water

FILLING

1 can almond paste

4 tablespoons butter or margarine

½ cup sugar

¼ teaspoon salt

2 large eggs

2 teaspoons vanilla extract

¼ cup all-purpose flour

1½ cups blueberries

1. **Prepare crust:** In a medium bowl, mix flour and salt. With pastry blender or two knives used scissor-fashion, cut in butter with shortening until mixture resembles coarse crumbs. Add water, 1 tablespoon at a time, mixing lightly with fork after each addition, until dough is just moist enough to hold together. Shape dough into a disk; wrap in plastic wrap and refrigerate for 30 minutes.

2. On a lightly floured surface, with floured rolling pin, roll dough into a 14-inch round. Ease dough round into an 11" by 1" round tart pan with removable bottom. Fold in overhang and press against side of tart pan to form a rim ⅛-inch above edge of pan. Refrigerate for 15 minutes to firm pastry slightly before baking.

3. Preheat oven to 375°F. Line the tart shell with foil and fill with pie weights, dried beans, or uncooked rice. Bake for 20 minutes; remove foil with weights and bake 8 to 10 minutes longer or until golden. Transfer pan to wire rack.

4. **Prepare blueberry-almond filling:** In a large bowl, with mixer on medium speed, beat almond paste, butter, sugar, and salt until evenly blended, scraping bowl frequently with rubber spatula (mixture will resemble coarse crumbs). Add eggs and vanilla. Increase speed to medium-high, and beat until blended. (It's okay if there are tiny lumps.) With spoon, stir in flour.

5. Pour almond mixture into warm tart shell; spread evenly. Scatter blueberries in an even layer over filling. Bake tart for 40 to 45 minutes, until golden. Cool tart in pan on wire rack. When cool, carefully remove side from pan.

Ginger-Apple-Walnut Crumble Pie

Ginger-spiced apples are buried beneath a warm, nutty
brown-sugar-and-almond crumble in this flavor-upgraded pie.

MAKES ONE 9-INCH PIE

1$^1/_4$ **cups plus 2 tablespoons
all-purpose flour, divided, plus
more for surface**

1 circle Basic Pie Dough (page 25)

$^1/_3$ **cup granulated sugar**

$^1/_2$ **teaspoon ground cinnamon**

2$^1/_2$ **tablespoons grated fresh
ginger, divided**

$^1/_2$ **teaspoon kosher salt, divided**

2$^1/_2$ **pounds Granny Smith,
Golden Delicious, or Pink Lady
apples, peeled and cut into
1-inch pieces**

$^3/_4$ **cup chopped walnuts**

$^1/_2$ **cup packed light brown sugar**

$^1/_2$ **cup unsalted butter, at room
temperature**

1. Preheat oven to 350°F. On a floured surface, roll dough to a 13-inch circle.
Transfer to a 9-inch pie plate, fold edges under, and align with the rim of the
plate; crimp.

2. Whisk together granulated sugar, cinnamon, 2 tablespoons flour,
1$^1/_2$ tablespoons ginger, and $^1/_4$ teaspoon salt. Add apples; toss to coat.
Transfer to pie plate. Freeze for 15 minutes.

3. Whisk together walnuts, brown sugar, 1$^1/_4$ cups flour, 1 tablespoon ginger,
and $^1/_4$ teaspoon salt. Work in butter until large clumps form; crumble
over apples.

4. Bake on a baking sheet until golden and bubbling, 60 to 70 minutes
(tenting with foil if crumble becomes too dark). Cool on a rack for at least
4 hours.

Double-Plum Almond Tart

"Double Plum" refers to the two types of plums (red and purple)
used to make this elegant almond-laced tart.

MAKES ONE 13-INCH TART

TART SHELL

1¼ cups all-purpose flour

¼ cup confectioners' sugar

¼ teaspoon salt

½ cup (1 stick) unsalted butter

1 large egg yolk

1 tablespoon cold water

FILLING

¼ cup almond paste

2 tablespoons unsalted butter

1 large egg

1½ tablespoons all-purpose flour

1 tablespoon sugar

2 ripe red plums

2 ripe purple plums

1 tablespoon sliced almonds

2 tablespoons apricot preserves,
melted

1. **Make the tart-shell dough:** In a food processor, pulse flour, sugar, and salt to mix. Add butter and pulse until mixture resembles small peas. Mix together egg yolk and water; with the machine running, add yolk mixture through the feed tube and process until the dough forms a ball.

2. Press the dough over the bottom and up the sides of a 13" by 3½" rectangular tart pan. Prick the bottom with a fork; freeze for 15 minutes.

3. Meanwhile, place an oven rack in the bottom position and preheat oven to 400°F.

4. **Make the filling:** In a food processor, process the almond paste until crumbled. Add butter, egg, flour, and sugar and process until smooth; pour into tart shell. Arrange slices of fruit in alternating rows, then sprinkle with almonds.

5. Bake until the tart is golden brown, about 30 minutes. Cool completely in pan on wire rack. Brush top with melted preserves. To serve, remove sides of tart pan; place tart on serving plate.

Old-Fashioned Pecan Pie

A light and flaky crust, plus brown sugar and molasses,
bring a rich new depth of flavor to this tried-and-true classic pie.

MAKES ONE 9-INCH PIE

Perfect Piecrust (page 22), unbaked

1 cup maple syrup

1 cup light brown sugar

½ cup heavy whipping cream

1 tablespoon molasses

4 tablespoons butter, cubed

½ teaspoon salt

6 large egg yolks, lightly beaten

2 cups pecan halves, lightly toasted

1. Roll out half the dough (one disk) on a lightly floured sheet of parchment paper to ¼-inch thickness (about a 12-inch circle). Fit into a 9-inch pie plate, crimping edges as desired. Refrigerate for 30 minutes to 1 hour.

2. Preheat oven to 425°F.

3. Combine maple syrup, light brown sugar, heavy whipping cream, and molasses in a 3½-quart saucepan. Cook over medium heat, stirring often, until sugar dissolves, about 3 minutes. Remove from heat; let cool 5 minutes. Whisk in butter and salt. Whisk in egg yolks.

4. Spread pecans evenly in prepared crust. Carefully pour syrup mixture over pecans.

5. Place in preheated oven and reduce heat to 325°F. Bake for 45 to 50 minutes, or just until filling is set and center jiggles slightly when gently shaken.

6. Cool completely on a wire rack.

Maple Granola Pecan Pie

Looking for a classic dessert with a twist? This decadent pecan pie promises a pop of flavor with the addition of maple syrup and pecan-coconut granola.

MAKES ONE 9-INCH PIE

1 cup regular oats

1/3 teaspoon ground cinnamon

6 tablespoons butter, melted

1 cup plus 2 tablespoons grade B maple syrup

1 1/2 cups pecan halves and pieces

1/2 cup sweetened flaked coconut

1/2 package refrigerated piecrusts (1 piecrust)

1/2 cup firmly packed brown sugar

2 teaspoons all-purpose flour

1/4 teaspoon salt

3 large eggs

2 teaspoons vanilla extract

1. Heat oven to 350°F. In a small bowl, stir together oats, cinnamon, 2 tablespoons melted butter, and 2 tablespoons maple syrup until blended. Spread oat mixture on a lightly greased baking sheet. Bake for 20 minutes or until oats begin to turn golden; remove from oven and stir in pecans and coconut. Bake 10 to 12 minutes more, or until pecans and coconut are lightly toasted. Remove from oven and cool completely on a wire rack, about 15 minutes.

2. Fit refrigerated piecrust into a 9-inch pie plate according to package directions; fold edges under and crimp as desired.

3. Whisk together brown sugar, flour, and salt until blended. Add eggs, vanilla, remaining 4 tablespoons melted butter, and remaining 1 cup maple syrup, whisking until blended. Spoon pecan mixture into prepared piecrust; carefully pour maple syrup mixture over pecan mixture.

4. Bake on lower oven rack for 35 to 40 minutes or until set. Remove from oven and cool completely on a wire rack, about 1 hour.

Chocolate-Pecan Tartlets

These tartlets are sweet and oh-so-rich, but worth the splurge for special occasions. Come Kentucky Derby time, revelers beat a path to Sweet Surrender Dessert Café for these buttery, miniature takes on the classic chocolate-pecan pie known as the Derby Pie. For a little extra kick, owner Jessica Haskell advises soaking the pecans in bourbon the night before you bake the tartlets.

MAKES 10 TARTLETS

CRUST

2 cups (4 sticks) unsalted butter, chilled and cut into ½-inch cubes, plus more for greasing pans

5 cups all-purpose flour

1 cup ice water

FILLING

8 ounces pecan halves

1 cup sugar

1 tablespoon all-purpose flour

4 large eggs

1 cup light corn syrup

1 tablespoon unsalted butter, melted

⅔ cup semisweet chocolate chips

1. **For the crust:** Butter ten 3½-inch tartlet pans; set aside. In a medium bowl, cut the butter into the flour using a pastry cutter, 2 knives, or your fingers until the mixture resembles coarse meal with bean-size bits mixed in. Slowly drizzle in the ice water and mix just until a dough forms (you may not need all the water). Do not overwork.

2. On a lightly floured surface, roll out half the dough to ⅛-inch thickness. With a sharp knife, cut five 6-inch circles and fit them into the prepared pans. Trim the excess dough from the rims, saving the scraps. Repeat the process with the remaining half of the dough. Gather and reroll the scraps as needed. Place the tartlet pans on 2 baking sheets; set aside. Preheat the oven to 325°F.

3. **For the filling:** Chop enough of the pecans to make ⅔ cup and set nearby; reserve the remaining pecan halves. In a large bowl, mix together the sugar and flour. Whisk in the eggs, corn syrup, and butter until combined. Mix in the chopped pecans and the chocolate chips. Divide the mixture evenly among the prepared tartlet pans. Arrange the pecan halves on top of the filling.

4. Bake until golden on the edges and set in the center, about 25 minutes. Transfer to a wire rack to cool completely, and then chill overnight so that the tartlets fully set.

Savory Pies

Savory Gruyère-Apple Tarts

The creamy, nutty Gruyère makes the perfect match for the dually sweet and tart Braeburn apples.

MAKES 4 TARTS

2 tablespoons unsalted butter

1 small yellow onion, finely diced

1 sheet frozen puff pastry, thawed

2 large Braeburn apples, peeled, cored, and thinly sliced

4 ounces Gruyère cheese, chopped into ¼-inch cubes

1. Preheat oven to 400°F. In a small skillet over medium heat, melt 1 tablespoon butter. Sauté onion until softened, about 5 minutes. Set aside.

2. Meanwhile, on a work surface, roll out puff pastry into a 13" by 10" rectangle. Cut dough into four 6½" by 5" rectangles. Using a sharp knife, score 4 lines to create a ½-inch border all the way around each tart. Transfer to a parchment-lined baking pan.

3. Divide half of the onion mixture among the tarts. Layer apples in 3 slightly overlapping rows on each. Top with remaining onion mixture and cheese. Dot with remaining butter. Bake tarts until apples are tender and cheese is golden, about 20 minutes.

Pesto-Ricotta Quiche

This is the perfect pie to make when fresh basil is abundant. And the crust could not be easier – store-bought phyllo dough, rolled very thin and layered to create a light and flaky pastry, is pressed into a pie tin to create a casual crust for the egg and cheese filling.

MAKES ONE 9-INCH PIE

6 tablespoons unsalted butter

1 large leek, trimmed, washed, and thinly sliced

2 large eggs

2 large egg whites

¼ cup heavy cream

1 cup ricotta

½ cup grated Parmesan cheese

3 tablespoons Chunky Chopped Pesto (recipe below)

2 tablespoons finely chopped fresh parsley leaves

¼ teaspoon salt

¼ teaspoon ground black pepper

8 frozen phyllo sheets, thawed

1. Preheat the oven to 375°F. Lightly butter a 9-inch pie pan and set aside. Melt 2 tablespoons butter in a medium-sized skillet over medium-high heat. Add the leeks and cook, stirring often, until soft, 5 to 7 minutes. Transfer to a large bowl to cool.

2. Meanwhile, whisk the eggs, egg whites, and cream together in a medium-sized bowl and add to the leeks, along with the ricotta, Parmesan, pesto, parsley, salt, and pepper. Stir to combine and set aside. Melt the remaining 4 tablespoons butter in a small bowl.

3. Lay one sheet of phyllo in the prepared pie pan. Brush the phyllo with melted butter, leaving a 1½-inch rim un-brushed. Lay a second sheet of phyllo on the first and butter it the same way. Repeat with the remaining sheets of phyllo.

4. Using kitchen shears, trim the edges of the phyllo to roughly conform to the shape of the pie pan, then pour in the filling. Brush the top of the phyllo rim with butter, and bake until the edges are golden brown and the filling is set, about 40 minutes. Transfer to wire rack to cool. Serve warm.

CHUNKY CHOPPED PESTO

7½ cups fresh basil leaves

1½ cups extra-virgin olive oil

3 cloves garlic

1 teaspoon coarse salt

1½ teaspoon ground black pepper

¾ cup toasted pine nuts

¾ cup grated Parmesan cheese

Puree the basil, oil, garlic, salt, and pepper in a food processor. Add the pine nuts and Parmesan, and pulse until the nuts are finely chopped.

Mushroom and Leek Tart

Thanks to the packaged puff pastry, this springtime tart is a cinch to make! The mushrooms bring a bold flavor that is complemented by the leeks, Dijon mustard, and Parmesan cheese.

MAKES TWO 12-INCH TARTS

3 tablespoons unsalted butter, divided

1 pound mushrooms (such as cremini and button), thickly sliced

1 large leek (white and light green parts only), sliced into ½-inch-thick rings

2 garlic cloves, chopped

2 teaspoons chopped fresh thyme, plus more whole leaves for garnish

Kosher salt and freshly ground black pepper

All-purpose flour, for work surface

½ (17.3-ounce) package puff pastry, thawed

2 tablespoons Dijon mustard

1 ounce Parmesan cheese, grated

1 large egg, beaten

1. Preheat oven to 400°F.

2. Melt 2 tablespoons butter in a large skillet over medium-high heat. Add mushrooms and sauté until golden brown, 6 to 8 minutes. Remove mushrooms to a plate; reserve skillet. Add remaining tablespoon butter, leek, garlic, and thyme to reserved skillet and sauté until leek is wilted, 2 to 4 minutes. Stir in mushrooms and season with salt and pepper.

3. Lightly flour work surface. Unfold pastry and roll, sealing seams if necessary, into a 10" by 12" rectangle. Cut pastry into two 5" by 12" rectangles and place on 2 parchment-lined baking sheets. Lightly prick the dough with a fork, leaving a ¼-inch border all around. Spread the mustard on the dough, inside the border. Sprinkle with Parmesan and top with mushroom mixture. Brush edges of pastry with egg.

4. Bake until edges are golden brown, 16 to 18 minutes. Garnish with thyme.

Fig and Brie Turnovers

These flaky, phyllo-wrapped turnovers pair nicely with a crisp white wine. For a terrific variation, try adding blue cheese to the filling instead of Brie.

MAKES 10 TURNOVERS

1 tablespoon unsalted butter

2 medium onions, chopped (about 2 cups)

3/4 cup apple cider

1 tablespoon honey

3/4 cup dried figs, coarsely chopped

8 frozen phyllo sheets, thawed

1/4 teaspoon ground black pepper

8 ounces Brie cheese, cut into pieces

Olive oil cooking spray

1. In a large nonstick skillet, melt the butter over medium heat. Add the onions and cook, stirring occasionally, until they are golden brown and caramelized, 20 to 30 minutes. Set aside.

2. Meanwhile, hydrate the figs: In a small saucepan over medium-high heat, bring the cider and honey to a boil. Remove the pan from the heat, add the figs, and cover. Allow the figs to sit until softened, about 30 minutes. Drain and set aside. Position a rack in the top third of the oven and preheat to 375°F.

3. Remove the phyllo from the package and cover it with a dampened dish towel. Place a sheet of phyllo on the work surface, spray it with cooking spray, and cover it with a sheet of plastic wrap, pressing to allow the spray to penetrate the dough. Remove the plastic wrap and layer on another sheet of phyllo. Repeat with the remaining sheets of phyllo. Sprinkle the top layer of dough evenly with pepper.

4. Cut the phyllo dough lengthwise into 5 equal strips, then cut each strip in half horizontally (this task is easiest with a pizza wheel). Place 1 1/2 tablespoons cheese at the bottom of each strip, top it with 2 teaspoons figs and 1 tablespoon caramelized onion; fold each strip around the filling into a triangle shape, as you would fold a flag.

5. Bake the turnovers for 20 minutes, or until the tops are lightly browned. Transfer to a wire rack to cool completely. Serve warm.

Wild Mushroom Tart

This flavorful, savory tart makes a satisfying supper. Serve it at room temperature alongside a simple green salad tossed in vinaigrette.

CRUST

1½ cups all-purpose flour

½ teaspoon salt

½ cup (1 stick) butter, chilled and cut into small pieces

2 to 3 tablespoons ice water

FILLING

1 cup unfiltered apple cider

¾ cup dried porcini mushrooms

3 tablespoons olive oil

⅓ cup chopped shallots

8 ounces white mushrooms, sliced

4 ounces wild mushrooms (such as cremini, shiitake, or chanterelle), sliced

¼ cup Calvados, applejack, or hard cider

½ cup chopped fresh flat-leaf parsley

½ teaspoon salt

¼ teaspoon ground black pepper

4 large eggs

¾ cup heavy cream

1 cup grated smoked mozzarella or smoked Gouda cheese

½ cup grated Parmesan cheese

1. **For the crust:** In a food processor fitted with a metal blade, combine the flour, salt, and butter. Pulse until the mixture resembles coarse meal, about 6 pulses. With the processor running, add the ice water, 1 tablespoon at a time, just until the dough comes together, no longer than 15 seconds. Gather the dough into a rough ball, flatten it into a 7-inch disk, and wrap it in plastic wrap. Refrigerate for at least 1 hour or up to 24 hours. Preheat the oven to 375°F.

2. Roll out the dough to an 11-inch round between 2 sheets of plastic wrap. Remove the top sheet of plastic wrap and invert the round into a 9-inch tart pan with a removable bottom. Carefully peel off the remaining sheet of plastic wrap. Tuck the dough into the pan and trim the edges so they are even with the top of the pan. Freeze the shell for 10 minutes. Line the bottom of the prepared pan with waxed paper or foil and fill it with pie weights or dried beans. Bake for 20 minutes. Transfer to a wire rack to cool; remove the weights and paper. Leave the oven on.

3. **For the filling:** In a small saucepan or microwaveable container, bring the cider to a boil. Pour the hot liquid over the dried porcini mushrooms and let them hydrate for 10 minutes.

4. Heat the oil in a large skillet and sauté the shallots and fresh mushrooms for about 10 minutes. Add the hydrated porcini mushrooms, along with their soaking liquid, and the Calvados. Cook over medium-low heat until almost all the liquid is absorbed, about 15 minutes. Stir in the parsley, salt, and pepper.

5. In a large bowl, combine the eggs, cream, and cheeses. Stir in the mushroom mixture. Pour the filling into the prepared crust.

6. Bake the tart until a toothpick inserted in the center comes out clean and the top has browned, 30 to 35 minutes. Transfer to a wire rack to cool slightly before removing the rim from the tart pan. Serve warm. (The tart may be prepared 1 day ahead and refrigerated. Reheat in a 350°F oven for 20 to 25 minutes.)

Caramelized-Onion and Gruyère Tarts

These ready-to-bake tarts are perfect for drop-in visitors. You need only plan ahead for reheating time. Add a sprinkling of fresh herbs, a bottle of wine, and a simple green salad to make the meal feel special.

MAKES 8 TARTS

3 cups grated Gruyère cheese (about 10 ounces)

8 ounces (1 package) cream cheese, softened

1 tablespoon Dijon mustard

1 tablespoon chopped fresh oregano

$3/4$ teaspoon ground black pepper

2 tablespoons unsalted butter

2 large sweet yellow onions, sliced $1/4$-inch thick (2 cups)

2 tablespoons fresh thyme

1 recipe Quick Puff Pastry (page 26)

$1/2$ cup Kalamata olives, sliced

1. Preheat the oven to 400°F (if you plan to freeze the tarts, do not preheat, and omit step 3 below). Mix the Gruyère, cream cheese, mustard, oregano, and pepper in a small bowl and set aside. Melt the butter in a large skillet over medium-low heat, add the onions, and cook, stirring occasionally, until dark brown and caramelized, about 1 hour. Stir in the thyme and set aside.

2. With a sharp knife, cut the puff pastry dough into 8 equal-sized pieces. Roll each piece out into an 8″ by 6″ rectangle. Spread about $1/4$ cup of the cheese mixture on each piece of dough, leaving a $1/2$-inch border. Top with $1/4$ cup caramelized onions and 1 tablespoon olives. Place the tarts on parchment-lined baking pans.

3. Bake the tarts for 10 minutes, then reduce the oven temperature to 375°F and continue baking until they are puffed and golden, about 12 minutes longer.

4. **To freeze the tarts before baking them:** Cover the tarts on the baking pan with plastic wrap and freeze until they are solid, about 2 hours. Wrap each tart securely in freezer paper or aluminum foil; stack them in an airtight container. Store the frozen tarts for up to 2 months. To serve, bake the frozen tarts at 400°F for 12 minutes, then reduce the oven temperature to 375°F, and continue baking until puffed and golden, about 15 minutes longer.

Quiche Lorraine Empanadas

No utensils necessary! These handheld quiches are a cinch to make,
and you can whip them up even faster if you substitute store-bought pie dough.
Serve them with a simple green salad for a lazy Sunday brunch.

MAKES 6 EMPANADAS

2 cups all-purpose flour

$3/4$ teaspoon salt

11 tablespoons unsalted butter

$1/3$ cup ice water

$1/4$ cup chopped yellow onion

3 large eggs

2 large egg yolks

$1/2$ cup plus 3 tablespoons heavy cream

$1/4$ teaspoon ground black pepper

$1/4$ teaspoon freshly grated nutmeg

$1 1/2$ cups grated Gruyère cheese

6 slices thickly cut bacon, cooked and chopped

1. Pulse the flour, $1/2$ teaspoon salt, and 10 tablespoons butter in the bowl of a food processor fitted with a metal blade until the mixture resembles coarse meal. Drizzle in the ice water in a steady stream, just until a dough forms (you may not need to use all the water). Turn the dough out of the bowl and pat into a disk. Wrap it with plastic wrap and chill for 1 hour.

2. Heat the remaining 1 tablespoon butter in a medium frying pan over medium heat. Add the onion and cook until soft, about 4 minutes. Reduce the heat to medium-low. In a medium bowl, whisk together the eggs, egg yolks, all but 1 tablespoon cream, remaining $1/4$ teaspoon salt, pepper, and nutmeg. Add 1 cup Gruyère and pour the egg mixture into the pan with the onions. Whisk until the eggs just begin to set, 8 to 10 minutes. Transfer the mixture to a bowl and stir to cool. Add the bacon and set aside.

3. Preheat the oven to 425°F and line a baking pan with parchment paper. Divide the dough into 6 equal pieces, and roll each into an 8-inch round. Divide the filling among the dough rounds and sprinkle the remaining $1/2$ cup Gruyère over all. Fold the dough over and crimp the edges with the tines of a fork to seal. Transfer the empanadas to the prepared baking pan. Brush them with the remaining 1 tablespoon cream and bake until golden, about 20 minutes. Transfer to a wire rack to cool. Serve warm.

Turkey and Autumn Vegetable Tart

A medley of fall flavors, this hearty supper tart puts your leftover Thanksgiving turkey to delicious use. During other times of the year, use precooked dark-meat turkey from the supermarket.

CRUST

1½ cups all-purpose flour, unsifted

1 teaspoon fresh thyme leaves

½ teaspoon salt

½ cup vegetable shortening, chilled

4 to 5 tablespoons ice water

FILLING

1 large (¾-pound) sweet potato, peeled and cut into 1-inch cubes

1 (10-ounce) package frozen Brussels sprouts, thawed

2 cups cooked turkey, cut into 1-inch pieces

4 tablespoons (½ stick) unsalted butter

1 medium onion, chopped

2 tablespoons all-purpose flour

⅔ cup turkey or chicken broth

⅔ cup whole milk

¼ teaspoon salt

⅓ cup dried unseasoned breadcrumbs

¼ teaspoon fresh thyme leaves

1. **For the thyme crust:** In a medium bowl, combine the flour, thyme, and salt. Cut in the shortening using a pastry blender, 2 knives, or your fingers until the mixture resembles very coarse meal. Add the ice water, 1 tablespoon at a time, tossing with a fork until the mixture holds together when lightly pressed. Shape into a disk, wrap in waxed paper, and refrigerate until chilled, about 30 minutes.

2. Preheat the oven to 400°F. Roll the dough between 2 sheets of floured waxed paper into a 12-inch round. Remove the top sheet of waxed paper and invert the pastry into a 10-inch tart pan with removable bottom, allowing the excess to extend over the edge. Peel off the remaining sheet of waxed paper. Fold the excess pastry inside so that it is even with the rim of the pan; press the pastry against the side to an even thickness. With a fork, pierce the bottom of the pastry 10 to 12 times to prevent shrinkage during baking. Line the pastry with foil and fill with pie weights or dried beans. Bake the pastry for 15 minutes, and then remove the foil and beans. Bake 10 to 15 minutes longer, or until the bottom of the pastry is golden and crisp. Transfer to a wire rack to cool completely.

3. **Meanwhile, prepare the filling:** In a heavy 2-quart saucepan, combine the sweet potatoes with enough water to cover. Heat to boiling over high heat. Reduce the heat to low; cover and cook for 10 minutes. Add the Brussels sprouts and cook for 5 minutes longer. Drain well and transfer to a bowl. Fold the turkey into the sweet potatoes and Brussels sprouts; set aside.

4. Wipe out the saucepan and melt the butter in it. Set aside 2 tablespoons of the melted butter in a small bowl. Add the onion to the butter remaining in the saucepan and sauté until golden. Stir in the flour until completely incorporated. Gradually stir in the broth, milk, and salt. Heat to boiling, stirring constantly, until the sauce thickens.

5. **Assemble and bake the tart:** Fold ½ cup sauce into the turkey and vegetable mixture. Spoon the filling into the pastry shell and top with the remaining sauce. Combine the reserved melted butter with the breadcrumbs and thyme. Sprinkle the crumb mixture over the filling. Bake the tart until the crumbs brown, 8 to 10 minutes. Transfer to a wire rack to cool slightly before removing the rim of the pan. Serve warm.

Simple Shepherd's Pie

This cozy, cold-weather classic promises a hearty, belly-filling dinner. Ground turkey pairs deliciously with the veggies and offers full flavor for a fraction of the calories and fat.

MAKES ONE 10-INCH PIE

2 tablespoons extra-virgin olive oil

3 small carrots, chopped

1 cup frozen pearl onions

1 pound lean ground turkey

1 tablespoon all-purpose flour

1 cup frozen peas

2¹/₂ teaspoons chopped fresh rosemary

Salt and freshly ground black pepper

³/₄ cup low-sodium chicken broth

3 cups leftover mashed potatoes

1. Preheat oven to 400°F. In a large pan, heat olive oil over medium heat. Add carrots and onions and cook until soft, about 5 minutes. Add turkey and cook, breaking up meat with a wooden spoon, until browned, about 6 minutes. Stir in flour and cook 3 minutes more. Stir in peas and rosemary. Season with salt and pepper. Transfer to a 9- to 10-inch deep-dish pie pan.

2. Spread mashed potatoes atop turkey mixture. Bake until golden on top and heated through, about 25 minutes.

Prosciutto and Fig Crostata

Prosciutto and figs are a classic Italian combination, so why not use them as crostata toppers? The saltiness of the prosciutto is beautifully balanced by the deep sweetness of the figs.

MAKES ONE 12-INCH CROSTATA

4 ounces dried Black Mission figs

¼ cup fresh lemon juice

1 tablespoon fresh thyme leaves

2 cloves garlic

½ teaspoon coarse sea salt

1 (9-inch) store-bought, unroll-and-fill piecrust, or ¼ recipe Grandma's Pie Dough (page 25)

4 ounces (½ package) cream cheese, softened

2 ounces prosciutto, cut into ½-inch-wide strips

1 large egg white

1. Preheat the oven to 425°F. Place the figs, lemon juice, thyme, garlic, and salt in the bowl of a food processor fitted with a metal blade and process to a smooth paste. Set aside.

2. Roll the dough into a 13-inch circle on a lightly floured surface. Transfer the round to a baking sheet and gently spread the cream cheese onto the dough, leaving a ¾-inch-wide border. Spread the fig mixture over the cream cheese and fold the border edge over the fig mixture to form the crostata.

3. Top the crostata with the prosciutto strips and lightly brush the folded edge of the dough with the egg white. Bake until golden, about 15 minutes. Cool on the sheet for 10 to 15 minutes before serving.

Tomato and Cheese Pie

This pie takes a savory turn with a ripe tomato-and-cheese filling seasoned with fresh chopped basil.

MAKES ONE 9-INCH PIE

4 medium plum tomatoes

1 (9-inch) store-bought deep-dish pie shell, prebaked according to package directions

1 cup finely chopped white onion

1/2 teaspoon salt

1/2 teaspoon ground black pepper

2 tablespoons chopped fresh basil

1/2 cup mayonnaise

1/2 cup grated Parmesan cheese

1 cup grated Cheddar cheese

1. Preheat the oven to 375°F. Cut 6 nice slices from one of the tomatoes and set them aside for garnish. Halve the remaining tomatoes, remove the seeds, and cut each half into about 6 wedges.

2. Arrange half of the tomato wedges in the bottom of the pie shell. Sprinkle with 1/2 cup onion, 1/4 teaspoon each salt and pepper, and 1 tablespoon basil.

3. Stir together the mayonnaise, Parmesan, and Cheddar in a small bowl, and dab half of this mixture over the onion layer. Repeat the layering to use the remaining tomatoes, onion, salt, pepper, and basil. Add the remaining mayonnaise mixture. Arrange the reserved tomato slices in a pinwheel design at the center of the pie.

4. Bake for 30 to 40 minutes, until golden brown. If the crust starts to overbrown, cover the edges with aluminum foil. Transfer to a wire rack to cool for 20 minutes. Serve warm.

Tomato and Camembert Tart

In this show-stopping tart, flaky pastry crust plays host to Gruyère and Camembert cheeses, sliced plum tomatoes, and a fragrant herb oil.

MAKES ONE 11-INCH TART

1½ cups all-purpose flour

6 tablespoons unsalted butter, chilled and cut into ½-inch pieces

½ teaspoon salt

½ teaspoon coarsely ground black pepper

2 to 3 tablespoons plus ½ cup extra-virgin olive oil

1 tablespoon water

1 tablespoon Dijon mustard

½ cup grated Gruyère cheese

4 plum tomatoes, seeds removed and cut into ½-inch slices

6 ounces Camembert cheese, cut into ⅛-inch strips

¼ cup fresh parsley, chopped

1 teaspoon fresh rosemary, finely chopped

1 tablespoon fresh thyme leaves

1 small bay leaf, finely crumbled

1 clove garlic, minced

1. Combine the flour, salt, and pepper; cut in the butter using a pastry blender, 2 knives, or your fingers until the mixture resembles coarse meal. Using a fork, mix in 2 tablespoons of the oil and the water, tossing just until the mixture begins to cling together. If necessary, add an additional table-spoon oil. Form the dough into a disk, wrap it in plastic wrap, and chill for 30 minutes.

2. Preheat the oven to 375°F and place the rack in the middle position. On a lightly floured surface, roll the chilled dough into a 14-inch circle and fit into an 11-inch tart pan with a removable bottom.

3. Spread the mustard over the bottom of the tart shell. Sprinkle the Gruyère evenly over the mustard and arrange the tomato and Camembert slices in alternation over the Gruyère.

4. In a small bowl, mix the remaining ½ cup olive oil, all the herbs, and the garlic, and brush two-thirds of the mixture over the tart. Bake for 35 minutes. Brush the tart with the remaining herb oil; transfer to a wire rack to cool slightly before removing the rim from the tart pan. Serve warm.

Chicken Potpie Turnovers

This portable version of a tried-and-true chicken classic promises all the flavors of the original—without the fork! Using pre-made empanada dough instead of piecrust saves time, as well as 9 grams of fat and 88 calories.

MAKES 8 TURNOVERS

1½ **pounds boneless, skinless chicken breasts**

2 **cups plus 1 tablespoon low-fat milk**

5 **sprigs thyme**

Salt and freshly ground black pepper

1 **tablespoon olive oil**

5 **shiitake mushrooms, sliced**

2 **medium carrots, chopped**

1 **small onion, chopped**

5 **ounces frozen green peas (about 1 cup)**

1 **tablespoon cornstarch**

1 **egg white**

8 **(7-inch) frozen empanada dough disks, thawed**

1. In a large saucepan over medium heat, bring chicken, 2 cups milk, 3 sprigs thyme, and ³/₄ teaspoon each salt and pepper to a simmer. Continue to simmer until chicken is cooked, 15 to 20 minutes, flipping halfway through. Transfer chicken to a cutting board and cool. Dice meat and set aside. Strain hot milk from saucepan and set aside 1 cup. Discard the remainder of contents.

2. Preheat oven to 400°F. Meanwhile, in a large nonstick skillet over medium-high heat, heat oil. Sauté mushrooms until soft, about 4 minutes. Add carrots and onion, reduce heat to medium, and cook until carrots are soft, about 10 minutes. Season with salt and pepper. Remove leaves from remaining thyme sprigs and add to skillet, along with peas and reserved chicken and milk; bring to a simmer.

3. In a small dish, stir together cornstarch and 3 tablespoons cold water. Add to skillet and stir over high heat until mixture thickens, 2 to 3 minutes. Remove skillet from heat and set aside.

4. In a small bowl, lightly beat egg white and remaining 1 tablespoon milk. Place empanada disks on 2 parchment paper-lined baking pans. Divide chicken filling among empanada disks, leaving ¹/₂-inch boarders around edges. Dampen edges with egg wash and fold dough over to create turnovers. Crimp edges with a fork to seal. Lightly brush tops of turnovers with egg wash. Bake until crusts are golden brown, about 15 minutes, turning pans halfway through.

INDEX

PHOTOGRAPHY CREDITS

METRIC EQUIVALENTS CHARTS

THE RECIPES IN THIS BOOK USE THE STANDARD U.S. METHOD FOR MEASURING LIQUID AND DRY OR SOLID INGREDIENTS (TEASPOONS, TABLESPOONS, AND CUPS). THE INFORMATION ON THIS CHART IS PROVIDED TO HELP COOKS OUTSIDE THE UNITED STATES SUCCESSFULLY USE THESE RECIPES. ALL EQUIVALENTS ARE APPROXIMATE.

METRIC EQUIVALENTS FOR DIFFERENT TYPES OF INGREDIENTS

A standard cup measure of a dry or solid ingredient will vary in weight depending on the type of ingredient. A standard cup of liquid is the same volume for any type of liquid. Use the following chart when converting standard cup measures to grams (weight) or milliliters (volume).

Standard Cup	Fine Powder (e.g., flour)	Grain (e.g., rice)	Liquid Granular (e.g., sugar)	Solids (e.g., butter)	Liquid (e.g., milk)
1	140 g	150 g	190 g	200 g	240 ml
3/4	105 g	113 g	143 g	150 g	180 ml
2/3	93 g	100 g	125 g	133 g	160 ml
1/2	70 g	75 g	95 g	100 g	120 ml
1/3	47 g	50 g	63 g	67 g	80 ml
1/4	35 g	38 g	48 g	50 g	60 ml
1/8	18 g	19 g	24 g	25 g	30 ml

USEFUL EQUIVALENTS FOR LIQUID INGREDIENTS BY VOLUME

1/4 tsp =				1 ml
1/2 tsp =				2 ml
1 tsp =				5 ml
3 tsp =	1 tblsp =		1/2 fl oz =	15 ml
	2 tblsp =	1/8 cup =	1 fl oz =	30 ml
	4 tblsp =	1/4 cup =	2 fl oz =	60 ml
	5 1/3 tblsp =	1/3 cup =	3 fl oz =	80 ml
	8 tblsp =	1/2 cup =	4 fl oz =	120 ml
	10 2/3 tblsp =	2/3 cup =	5 fl oz =	160 ml
	12 tblsp =	3/4 cup =	6 fl oz =	180 ml
	16 tblsp =	1 cup =	8 fl oz =	240 ml
	1 pt =	2 cups =	16 fl oz =	480 ml
	1 qt =	4 cups =	32 fl oz =	960 ml
			33 fl oz =	1000 ml = 1 L

USEFUL EQUIVALENTS FOR DRY INGREDIENTS BY WEIGHT

(To convert ounces to grams, multiply the number of ounces by 30.)

1 oz =	1/16 lb =	30 g
4 oz =	1/4 lb =	120 g
8 oz =	1/2 lb =	240 g
12 oz =	3/4 lb =	360 g
16 oz =	1 lb =	480 g

USEFUL EQUIVALENTS FOR COOKING/OVEN TEMPERATURES

	Farenheit	Celcius	Gas Mark
Freeze Water	32° F	0° C	
Room Temp.	68° F	20° C	
Boil Water	212° F	100° C	
Bake	325° F	160° C	3
	350° F	180° C	4
	375° F	190° C	5
	400° F	200° C	6
	425° F	220° C	7
	450° F	230° C	8

USEFUL EQUIVALENTS FOR LENGTH

(To convert inches to centimeters, multiply the number of inches by 2.5.)

1 in =			2.5 cm =
6 in =	1/2 ft =		15 cm =
12 in =	1 ft =		30 cm =
36 in =	3 ft =	1 yd =	90 cm =
40 in =			100 cm = 1 m